ELIZABETH I
OF
ENGLAND

ELIZABETH I
OF
ENGLAND

Kerrily Sapet

MORGAN
REYNOLDS
PUBLISHING

Greensboro, North Carolina

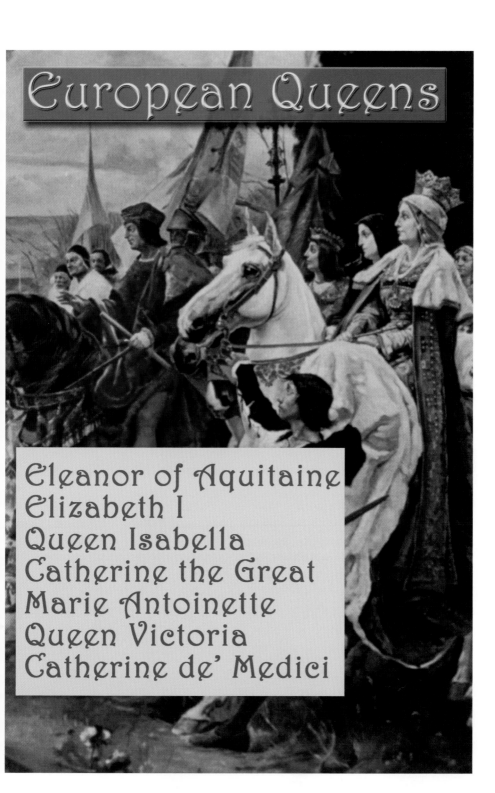

European Queens

Eleanor of Aquitaine
Elizabeth I
Queen Isabella
Catherine the Great
Marie Antoinette
Queen Victoria
Catherine de' Medici

ELIZABETH I OF ENGLAND

Copyright © 2005 by Kerrily Sapet

Library of Congress Cataloging-in-Publication Data

Sapet, Kerrily, 1972-
    Elizabeth I of England / Kerrily Sapet.— 1st ed.
        p. cm.
Includes bibliographical references and index.
    ISBN-13: 978-1-931798-70-9 (library binding)
    ISBN-10: 1-931798-70-2 (library binding)
1. Elizabeth I, Queen of England, 1533-1603. 2. Queens—Great
Britain—Biography. 3. Great Britain—History—Elizabeth, 1558-1603. I.
Title.
    DA357.S27 2005
    942.05'5'092—dc22

                    2005011930

Printed in the United States of America
First Edition

To my mother,
for her love of me and the Tudors

Contents

1

A LONELY PRINCESS

From the moment the tiny princess was born, she was the most talked about baby in England. But instead of referring to King Henry VIII's newest daughter with awe and respect, people laughed and called her a joke from God. Bonfires burned in the streets of London, as crowds drank barrels of the king's wine and reveled in his disappointment. Royal servants hastily changed the royal birth announcements from "prince" to "princess." King Henry had spent the last few anxious days trying to decide whether to name the baby Edward or Henry. This daughter was supposed to be a son.

Henry VIII desperately wanted a male heir. He thought only a son could fight off challenges to the Tudor family's claim to the throne.

Opposite: Queen Elizabeth I of England. *(National Portrait Gallery, London)*

A view of Greenwich Palace, where Elizabeth was born, from the Thames River. *(Ashmolean Museum, Oxford)*

Henry cancelled the jousting tournament planned to celebrate a male heir's birth and refused to attend the baby's christening. He had so little interest in her that he almost named her Mary, the same name given to his first daughter. Henry changed his mind at the last minute, and in a chapel perfumed with incense and bright with storytelling tapestries and handmade rugs, the infant princess was named Elizabeth, after her grandmother.

Elizabeth Tudor, born on September 7, 1533, at Greenwich Palace in London, faced adversity from the moment of her first breath. Not only was she the wrong sex, but her mother was the most despised woman in England.

Earlier that year, Elizabeth's father had divorced his popular wife of seventeen years, Catherine of Aragon. Only one of his six children with Catherine, their daugh-

Elizabeth's mother, Anne Boleyn. *(National Portrait Gallery, London)*

ter Mary, had survived birth. As Henry had two sons from mistresses, he reasoned that the inability to produce a son was Catherine's fault.

When Henry met Anne Boleyn in 1526, she was one of Catherine's maids of honor. The queen's maids helped her dress, served her meals, and kept her entertained and informed. During festivities, Anne and the other maids of honor dressed in elegant gowns and had the privilege of dancing with the king and his men. Raised at the French court, Anne was high-spirited, attractive, and fashionable—the opposite of Henry's pious, matronly wife.

With her long black hair and dancing, dark eyes,

Anne captivated Henry, but she refused to become his mistress. She did not want to be an outcast after bearing one of Henry VIII's illegitimate children, as her sister had before her. Anne would give Henry her heart but not her body until they were married. The wildly infatuated Henry began to work toward this purpose.

Henry decided that God had cursed his marriage to Catherine. Before becoming his wife, Catherine had been married, for less than six months, to Henry's brother Arthur. When Arthur died, Catherine swore that the marriage had never been consummated. Henry believed her. But now, all these years later, Catherine still had not produced a male heir, and Henry became convinced she had lied. The Bible forbid a man to marry his brother's wife. Henry believed God frowned upon his marriage and sent messengers to plead with Pope Clement for a papal dispensation to dissolve it.

Henry's request put Pope Clement in an agonizing posi-

Henry VIII's first wife, Catherine of Aragon, daughter of Isabella and Ferdinand of Spain.

Elizabeth's father, King Henry VIII.

tion. The most powerful man in Europe was Catherine's nephew, Charles V of the Hapsburg family. As Holy Roman Emperor, Charles controlled Spain, Germany, the Netherlands, portions of Italy, and the growing Spanish empire in America. His large army of mercenaries had invaded Rome only a few short years before, in 1527. Charles had been angry that Pope Clement had sided with the French against him in a war between France and Spain. That invasion had left thousands dead and had severely damaged the pope's prestige in Europe. Clement feared that Charles would attack Rome again if he allowed Henry to divorce Charles's aunt. To put pressure on the pope, Henry threatened to sever ties with the Catholic Church and Rome if he did not get what he wanted. The pope was in an impossible situation; it was said that he wept as he contemplated his choices. In the end, he refused Henry's plea for divorce.

An angry Henry had no choice but to follow through on his threat to break the English church away from papal control. He created the Church of England and placed himself at its head. He then stripped the English Catholic Church of its riches. He disbanded monasteries, confiscated church lands, and seized their treasures, enriching himself and his friends. Next, he bullied his new clergy into granting the divorce.

In one audacious sweep, Henry had cut his subjects off from the Catholic Church, the official church of Christian Europe. Pope Clement retaliated by excommunicating Henry, which expelled him from the church and, according to doctrine, condemned him to eternal damnation. Furthermore, according to the pope, Henry's subjects no longer owed him obedience. Another ruler could seize his kingdom, with the pope's blessing.

Popes had threatened kings with excommunication several times over the previous thousand years. There had long been tension between secular rulers and the church. Often the conflict was over who controlled the church's wealth in a country or who should decide who was made a bishop or a cardinal. Over the centuries, secular and spiritual leaders were able to work out compromises that avoided open conflict. Sometimes compromise was impossible, and at those times, if a conflict reached the boiling point, a papal threat of excommunication could force a ruler to submit.

Then in 1517, the unified world of European Christianity had been shattered by a single act of disobedience when an obscure German monk, Martin Luther, had nailed a long list of complaints to the door of the castle church in Wittenberg, Saxony, or present-day Germany. Luther's actions caught the attention of many who were frustrated with what they saw as a corrupt church. Luther quickly expanded his argument to attack some of the basic doctrines of Catholicism, and in a few short years the Protestant Reformation had begun. Over the first decades of the century, others would rise up to challenge the Catholic Church. The Frenchman John Calvin turned Geneva, Switzerland, into a Protestant stronghold and instituted his brand of the new faith that gave rise to what in England would come to be called Puritanism.

But Henry's break was motivated by more personal matters. He wanted to marry Anne Boleyn, who he hoped would soon produce a male heir. After years of waiting, their wedding was held on January 25, 1533. Many of Henry's subjects still loved the displaced Catherine and were not ready for a break from Catholicism, but they had no choice. There was no separation of church and state in the sixteenth century. The ruler decided the religion of his subjects. There were some who supported the break as the Protestant revolt spread throughout the continent; most critically, it had the support of a sizable number of the powerful English nobility.

Acceptance of the break from Rome, however, did not translate into love and support of the new queen. Most of her subjects despised her. She was called "the goggle-eyed whore" because of her prominent eyes. People pointed at the flags displaying Henry and Anne's initials intertwined and laughed, as their initials spelled out "HA.HA." Queen Anne responded by dressing her servants in clothing embroidered with the words, "Let them grumble, that is how it is going to be," in French.

After all this conflict and the dramatic, radical change the entire nation had undergone, Queen Anne's firstborn was a girl. The disappointment ran deep. One of the clergymen at Elizabeth's christening ceremony was asked if she was baptized in hot or cold water. "Hot," he replied, "but not hot enough." The disappointed Henry and Anne could only look forward to more children. The queen was still young. Henry even came to accept the new daughter, while Anne doted on her, ordering her expensive satin and silk dresses and colorful velvet sleeves.

When Elizabeth was three months old, in accordance with tradition, she was sent to live away from her parents. Elizabeth's miniature court was at Hatfield Royal Palace, about twenty miles north of London. Located in the airy countryside, Hatfield became one of several homes to Elizabeth. But the princess wasn't completely cut off from her parents. Anne visited her daughter frequently.

Elizabeth had the best of everything, down to the real gold and silver decorations on her cradle. The only thing she didn't have was a typical family life. Her parents visited when their duties permitted. Elizabeth's servants became her substitute family.

Occasionally, Elizabeth was brought to court to be shown off. Royal children were diplomatic assets. Henry used the lure of marriage to his daughter to build better relations with other countries. When Elizabeth was seven months old, she was almost betrothed to the king of France's son. She was even displayed naked to show she had no defects. But after months of negotiations, the plan was abandoned. The English demanded a yearly payment France did not want to make, and the French refused to send their king's son to England to be educated.

When Elizabeth was born, she replaced her seventeen-year-old half sister, Mary, in her father's affection and as the heiress to the throne of England. Upon Elizabeth's birth, an Act of Parliament stripped Mary of her title as the Princess of Wales. Mary was formally labeled a bastard because her parents' marriage no longer existed in the eyes of the law. Queen Anne, determined to demonstrate her new power, forced Mary to wait upon Elizabeth as a servant.

Mary was defiant and angry. She refused to curtsy to Elizabeth, declaring she "knew of no Princess in England but herself." Anne's treatment of Mary set the stage for years of mistrust and animosity between the two half sisters.

After Elizabeth's birth, Anne suffered three miscarriages in a row. The third time, the baby was a boy. Anne claimed she miscarried because she was upset when Henry was knocked unconscious during a jousting tournament. Courtiers whispered the true cause was a jealous rage after Anne caught Henry em-

Mary Tudor, Elizabeth's older half sister.

bracing Jane Seymour, one of her maids of honor. Either way, the miscarriage spelled disaster for Anne. Henry was disenchanted with her. She was vengeful with her enemies and cruel to her servants. Henry disliked Anne's flirtatious behavior and her tantrums over his mistresses. But Anne's worst sin was failing to give him a son.

Henry decided God would deny him a son as long as he remained married to Anne. He began to tell friends she had used witchcraft to trick him into marrying her. Henry wanted to be free of Anne so he could remarry and resume his quest for a male heir.

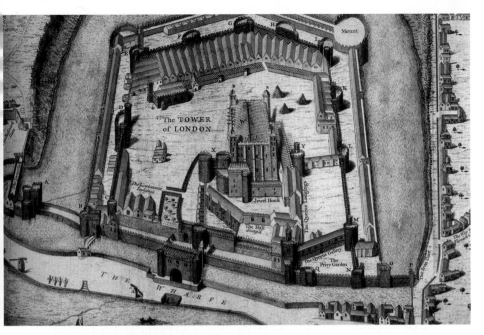

This sixteenth-century image of the infamous Tower of London shows the prison much as it looked on eve of Anne Boleyn's execution. *(British Library, London)*

Shortly before Elizabeth's third birthday, Henry had Anne arrested and imprisoned in the Tower of London, England's most important state prison and execution site. A massive stone castle surrounded by defensive towers and a moat, the over-four-hundred-year-old tower and its surrounding buildings also served as a mint, an armory, a jewel house, a royal residence, and a zoo. Conditions at the tower depended on the crime and the prisoner's social status. While some prisoners received visitors, read books, and walked in the courtyard, others were confined and tortured.

Anne was accused of plotting to kill Henry and of having affairs with four of the king's servants and her own brother. The five men were also arrested. Having an affair with the queen was a treasonous crime, punishable by death.

All but one of the men questioned swore to Anne's innocence. To end the torture of the rack, the musician Mark Smeaton confessed to an affair. No other evidence against Anne existed. After Smeaton's testimony, all five men were judged guilty. Anne was forced to watch as each man was beheaded.

The tales of Anne's crimes quickly became exaggerated. Henry claimed Anne had affairs with more than one hundred men. Meanwhile, Anne's maid Jane Seymour was given a house on the River Thames. Henry visited her nightly, his barge filled with minstrels and musicians, singing and playing loudly as they drifted along the water. Although few people felt sympathy for Anne, many felt Henry's actions, courting a third wife as the second awaited trial for her life, were wrong.

Anne was quickly convicted and sentenced to beheading. Her marriage to Henry was dissolved and declared invalid. She spent most of her final hours in prayer, swearing over and over she "had never been unfaithful to the king." On the morning of May 19, 1536, Anne was beheaded in front of hundreds of spectators and buried in a storage chest for bows and arrows, as no one had thought to order her a coffin. There was no church service. Before she died she wrote to Henry, begging him to take Elizabeth into his care. But Henry was busy, and to him, Elizabeth was an unpleasant reminder of Anne, the woman who had disappointed him so greatly. He banished Elizabeth from his sight.

Elizabeth's servants continued to care for the little

girl. As she grew, her image of Anne was shaped by whispered scraps of gossip she overheard from her servants. Elizabeth was raised to believe the king did no wrong. However, she was also learning love could be a dangerous weapon.

Elizabeth was without a stepmother for only ten days, until her father married Jane Seymour. Small, blonde-haired Jane was the opposite of Anne Boleyn. A quiet, shy woman in her late twenties, Jane offered Henry the hope of a male heir.

After Henry married Jane, Parliament declared Elizabeth illegitimate. She was barred from the succession, meaning she could no longer inherit Henry's throne. The Catholic Church already considered Elizabeth illegitimate, as it never recognized Henry's divorce from Catherine of Aragon. Mary had been disinherited; now it was Elizabeth's turn. Henry and Jane's children, male or female, would take precedence. Jane gave Henry the son he longed for on October 12, 1537. With her half brother Edward's birth, four-year-old Elizabeth was all but forgotten.

In the whirlwind of changes, Elizabeth's servants remained loyal and steady. She continued to live mainly at Hatfield. Elizabeth's governess, Lady Margaret Bryan, had to beg Henry for money to buy clothes when her nightgowns and underwear grew too small. Henry was preoccupied with his new wife and son. Sporadically, he ordered new clothing for Elizabeth and paid her household costs, but otherwise he largely ignored her. Money

The Royal Palace of Hatfield, Elizabeth's childhood home, no longer stands. The palace was rebuilt under James I in 1611 using parts of the original structure. Today, the building is a major British tourist attraction.

was a constant worry for Elizabeth. From her early childhood, she learned financial restraint.

Anne Boleyn had been accused of having affairs with other men, which led people to wonder whether Henry was Elizabeth's real father. Mary refused to acknowledge they had the same father, even though Elizabeth looked like Henry. Many people worried about young Elizabeth's morals because of her mother's reputation. Henry wanted her servants to be "ancient and sad persons" to prevent her from learning flirtatious behaviors. But while Elizabeth's servants loved her and she them, they were not an ordinary family. Always in the back of their minds was the knowledge that Elizabeth's fortunes could change. Just as Henry had squashed her rights as his heir, he could restore them at a whim. Elizabeth might be queen some day and wield considerable power.

Soon after Edward's birth, Jane Seymour died from complications of childbirth. Henry's fourth wife now was chosen for political reasons, rather than love. Catholic monarchs encircled England, and Henry needed friends among the Protestant nations. His popularity at home and abroad was waning as he became increasingly suspicious and temperamental. Potential wives quickly accepted other suitors; it was dangerous to become the wife of Henry VIII. Finally, Henry found Anne of Cleves— her home was one of the Protestant territories of Germany.

Henry agreed to marry her after viewing her portrait. Though he found her dull and unattractive when they finally met, he was by then politically obligated to go through with the marriage. But after six months, Henry divorced Anne, claiming he had never been able to consummate their marriage because she was so physically unappealing. Henry executed the official who had urged him to marry her. Anne agreed to the divorce and stayed in England. Although she spoke little English, she became a loving hon-

Anne of Cleves.

orary aunt to Henry's children. She and eight-year-old Elizabeth loved riding horses together.

Meanwhile, Elizabeth's father took a fifth wife, nineteen-year-old Catherine Howard. Catherine had been one of Anne of Cleves's maids of honor. Fifty-year-old Henry showered young Catherine with jewels and expensive dresses. A year and a half later, Henry discovered Catherine was sexually experienced before she married him, and adulterous after their marriage. Humiliated, he had her beheaded in 1542. Henry's rage became tears of self-pity in front of his council as he bemoaned his "ill luck in meeting such ill-conditioned wives."

By the age of nine, Elizabeth was sharp enough to understand the events around her. She confided in her friend Robert Dudley that she would never marry. Robert's father, John, was one of the most powerful men on Henry's council. His children often were allowed the privilege of playing with Edward and Elizabeth.

Elizabeth was fond of her brother Edward. When they were apart, she wrote letters to him in French and Latin and sent him presents she had made. The two children were bound together by the fact that both had lost their mothers.

Elizabeth continued to travel between several homes. With such a large court, garbage piled up in the large households, leading to a horrible stink. Elizabeth and her siblings moved so the house could be scrubbed and the vegetables and livestock supply could be replen-

Henry VIII is pictured in this famous family portrait flanked by his son, Edward, and the symbolic presence of Edward's mother, Jane Seymour, who in fact had died soon after Edward's birth. *(Windsor Castle)*

ished. Elizabeth grew to love Hatfield with its fresh country air, unlike polluted, crowded London. In the country, she was away from the diseases that often ravaged the cities.

If Elizabeth's parents hadn't given her a stable family, her father at least gave her a strong education. In the sixteenth century, children were seen as miniature adults. They were supposed to be serious, covering their mouths if they laughed. They also were to avoid frowning, yawning, wiggling, and smiling.

Most education involved physical punishment. Elizabeth's tutor, Roger Ascham, believed in a gentler approach. He praised Elizabeth as she learned, rather than threatening her. He made learning enjoyable, and she grew to love her lessons. Ascham passed on his talents in calligraphy and handwriting, and people admired Elizabeth's beautiful writing. He taught her history, architecture, astronomy, mathematics, geography, sewing, dancing, manners, horseback riding, and hunting.

Elizabeth was an intelligent, hard-working student, with a marvelous memory. She excelled in learning languages and became fluent in Greek, Latin, Italian, Spanish, French, Flemish, and even a bit of Welsh, knowing these languages would later help her speak directly with foreign ambassadors, rather than having to rely on translators. She also became a talented musician, playing the lute and the virginals, an early form of piano.

Although there were many learned ladies in England,

"the brightest star is my illustrious Lady Elizabeth," Ascham said.

When Henry married for the final time, in 1543, he chose wisely, both for himself and his children. He was drawn to Katherine Parr for her warm personality and intelligence. Henry was now grossly overweight. A foul-smelling ulcer on his leg made walking difficult. In the twice-widowed Katherine, Henry found a devoted, sensible wife who had experience nursing ailing husbands.

Katherine also welcomed Henry's children. At thirty-one years old, she was four years older than her new stepdaughter, Mary. The two women became friends. Katherine encouraged Mary to come to court, kept her abreast of court news, and lent her money. While making friends with Edward and Mary served Katherine well politically, she acted out of sheer kindness when she brought Elizabeth to court. Elizabeth often was treated as a poor relation because of her scandalous mother, and Katherine was

Henry VIII's last wife, Katherine Parr.

the first of Elizabeth's stepmothers to take an interest in her. Katherine made a home for the children at court. They had never all lived together on such a permanent basis. Katherine's efforts helped foster a closer family feeling between Henry and his children.

By February 1544, the aging Henry knew his end was near. He knew his chances of fathering more children were slim. Henry decided to restore Mary and Elizabeth to the succession. Although women, they were the only other heirs Henry had besides Edward. According to Henry's Act of Succession, Edward would be crowned first. If Edward died without heirs, Mary would become queen. Elizabeth was last in line, providing Mary had no children. Henry ignored the fact that Mary and Elizabeth had been declared illegitimate. Now it was possible, though unlikely, that Elizabeth might one day be crowned.

In July, an ailing Henry led an invasion into France, England's longtime enemy. France had worked to create an alliance with Scotland, located in the north of the British isle, as a way to encircle England. King James V of Scotland had married two French wives. Henry had hoped to arrange a marriage between Edward and James's daughter, Mary. But Scotland knew the marriage would result in English control, and in the end, Mary was promised to the eldest son of King Francis I of France. Facing a renewed French-Scottish alliance, Henry sought help from another foe of France: Holy Roman Emperor and king of Spain Charles V—the same Charles who refused to allow the pope to give Henry a divorce from Catherine of Aragon.

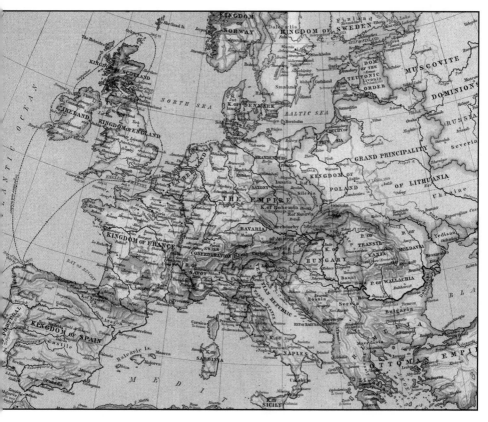
The various kingdoms of Europe during Tudor rule of England.

Although both France and Charles V's kingdoms remained officially Catholic, they had long been at war with each other over territories, including the Netherlands, the Pyrenees, and parts of Italy. France was surrounded by countries controlled by Charles: the Holy Roman Empire stood to the east, Spain to the southwest, the Spanish Netherlands to the north, and Spanish Mediterranean territories to the southeast. It is no surprise that Henry was successful on his last military campaign. Over the course of about two months, with Spanish help, Henry captured the port city of Boulogne, which France used to load ships with military supplies to be sent Scotland.

While he was away, Henry had named Katherine Parr as regent. This left her in charge of day-to-day affairs. Elizabeth observed powerful men bowing to an even more powerful queen. She would tuck these memories away.

Katherine, like many sixteenth-century Europeans, was interested in religious reform. Henry's break from the Catholic Church had sparked a religious revolution in England. The Bible was now available in English rather than just Latin, a radical departure for Europe. Now literate people could study and interpret the scripture themselves, instead of relying on priests. Katherine began to hold religious lectures in her private chambers. During these Protestant conferences, chaplains increased their attacks on Catholicism. What had started as a struggle between king and pope had now permeated the country. Arguments over religion and the correct interpretation of the Holy Bible were the hottest issues of the year. The Protestant ministers spoke out against even tolerating Catholic practices, such as holding mass in Latin and letting English subjects join the Roman Church. Theologically, they disputed the core Catholic belief that Jesus Christ was present during Mass, a service based on the Last Supper. Elizabeth quietly listened and learned.

Elizabeth was growing into a tall, striking young woman. She had her father's red hair, fair eyelashes and eyebrows, and hooked nose. She had her mother's long, thin, pale face and pointed chin, along with her dark, expressive eyes. Elizabeth could be quick-tempered and sharp-tongued when irritated, like her mother. But she was also self-confident and had a strong business sense, like her father.

Events in Elizabeth's childhood had made her cautious and secretive, traits that would serve her well in the future. Throughout her childhood, she kept her eyes open, learning and taking in the events swirling around her. Her father's many and difficult marriages left an especially deep impression.

On January 28, 1547, King Henry VIII died. Elizabeth was thirteen years old. For thirty-eight years, her father

Princess Elizabeth as a young teenager.

had ruled England. Already a legend, Henry would be remembered as a figure larger than life, having married six wives while mixing charm and terror equally. "He is a wonderful man and has wonderful people about him," said a French diplomat, adding that Henry also was "the most dangerous and cruel man in the world."

Elizabeth had both feared and been awed by Henry. Though they did not have a loving relationship, he had inspired her imagination. She learned the importance of the image of greatness from him. "She prides herself on her father and glories in him," said one ambassador years later.

Elizabeth and Edward were brought together and told of their father's death. Bursting into tears, they clung to each other. It was the last time they would be close. Nine-year-old Edward was taken to London to begin his reign as king of England.

As Edward ascended the throne, Elizabeth once again saw events in her life moving beyond her control. But never for a moment, throughout the difficulties she faced during her brother's and sister's reigns, would Elizabeth forget she was her father's daughter. She never let anyone else forget either.

2

TRAPPED

In 1547, just months after Henry's death, Elizabeth's stepmother, Katherine, married the dashing Thomas Seymour, the brother of Henry VIII's third wife, Jane. Thomas had already been King Edward's uncle and was now Elizabeth's stepfather. The Seymour family had close ties to the throne. Thomas's brother, Edward, had been named lord protector of England. The protector ruled and advised young King Edward until he was old enough to govern on his own.

Thomas Seymour was jealous of his brother's power. After Henry's death, Thomas Seymour had tried to marry Elizabeth or her sister Mary, but King Edward's council would not permit either match, seeing through Seymour's ambitious plans to snare the throne. Attracted by her money and prestige, Thomas Seymour settled on marrying Katherine, who was blindly in love with her handsome new husband.

The marriage gave Seymour direct access to Elizabeth, who had turned into a pretty teenaged girl. Elizabeth trusted Seymour and was flattered by his attentions. But soon, her stepfather's games became dangerous. He obtained a key to Elizabeth's bed-

Katherine Parr's second husband, Thomas Seymour.

chamber, letting himself in whenever he wanted. Seymour frequently surprised her in the morning, dressed only in his nightgown and slippers. He would lift back the curtains to her bed and try to jump in and tickle her while she hid under the sheets. One morning, Seymour tried to kiss her. Thereafter, Elizabeth avoided him by getting up early. She was dressed and studying when he came into her room. Seymour began to send her sexually suggestive notes.

Katherine sometimes joined Seymour's games, not realizing his true intentions with her stepdaughter. One day, as Elizabeth walked in the garden, Seymour pounced on her and tore the gown she was wearing into shreds. Elizabeth couldn't escape because Katherine was holding her.

Elizabeth's governess, Kat Ashley, seemed more amused than worried about Seymour's behavior. Elizabeth loved Kat as a mother, but while Kat was kindly and loyal, she was sometimes unwise. Kat liked Seymour and secretly wanted Elizabeth to marry him.

One day Katherine saw her husband holding Elizabeth in his arms. The games had gone too far. Angry and humiliated, she sent Elizabeth to live at Sir Anthony Denny's house. Denny had been King Henry's favorite servant and was married to Kat Ashley's sister. Elizabeth was embarrassed and physically sick with disgrace. She suffered violent headaches and pains behind her eyes from the emotional stress. Time and kind letters between Elizabeth and her stepmother mended their feelings. Then, in August of 1548, Katherine died in childbirth.

When Seymour lost his wife, he redoubled his efforts to marry Elizabeth. He was also plotting to overthrow her brother. Seymour attempted to kidnap Edward at gunpoint, but the king's guards foiled his plan and he was imprisoned in the Tower of London. Kat Ashley and Thomas Parry, who handled Elizabeth's finances, also were arrested. The three of them were accused of plotting to marry Elizabeth to Seymour and endangering King Edward. Elizabeth was suddenly in grave danger.

Gossip about Elizabeth and her stepfather ran wild.

One rumor said Elizabeth was imprisoned in the Tower, another that she was pregnant, and another that they already were married. Elizabeth, Ashley, and Parry were questioned for weeks. Fifteen-year-old Elizabeth loyally protected her two servants, those fixed points in her ever-changing world. Seymour was executed. A year later, Seymour's brother Edward would also be executed for treason. John Dudley, Robert's father, became the new lord protector. Elizabeth and her servants escaped the crisis, but Elizabeth's reputation was severely damaged.

Elizabeth had learned a valuable lesson about the importance of people's opinions. She also was drawing conclusions about relationships with men. Love often led to punishment, worries, and even death—either from conspiracy or childbirth.

Anxious to repair her image and her standing at Edward's court, Elizabeth began to cultivate the appearance of simplicity and innocence to combat the recent gossip. A born actress, she informed Edward and his council of her smallest activities, impressing upon them her desire for their approval. To appeal to Edward and his Protestant supporters, she dressed simply. While many ladies were in competition to be the most colorful and bejeweled, Elizabeth stood out dramatically with her sober black or white dresses and quiet, gentle manners. Elizabeth's tactics worked. She was invited to spend Christmas at Edward's court.

Young King Edward tried to live up to his father's reputation, but his thin, weak physique and high, boyish

The child king, Edward VI of England.

voice undercut his efforts. Young Edward was easily swayed by his councilors. Under their influence, he was a passionate Protestant who despised the Catholic Church.

While Elizabeth and Edward held similar religious views, their half sister Mary was devoutly Catholic. According to Henry VIII's will, if Edward died without any heirs, Mary was next in line for the throne, regardless of her religion. Until Edward married and had children, his Protestant council worried their frail boy-king might die and leave them with a Catholic ruler. Fearing the worst, Edward's advisors began a campaign to make Elizabeth the preferred successor to the throne. When Elizabeth was invited to Christmas, she entered London escorted by one hundred of the king's horses.

Back home at Hatfield, Elizabeth lived modestly. Her table was supplied with meats, eggs, fruit, and grains from Hatfield's working farm. Friends brought luxuries sometimes, such as swan and partridge. Local people left her gifts of apples or peas. The farm produced wool, leather, candles, and soap for the household. Elizabeth enjoyed playing music, reading, sewing, or hunting if the weather was good. If not, she often paced up and down or would lie, frustrated, in her bed. Living quietly was difficult and left her too much time to wonder whether her destiny would be to rule England, to be married off as a political pawn, or to live out her days as a spinster princess, left waiting.

In the spring of 1552, King Edward contracted measles. Although he recovered, his health steadily declined throughout the year. By Christmas it was clear he had tuberculosis, an incurable, infectious lung disease.

As Edward coughed up blood, his advisors coerced him into changing the order of succession. Lord Protector Dudley, for his own reasons, wanted both Mary and Elizabeth to be excluded as heirs to the throne. Mary was Catholic and would reestablish England as a Catholic country. Elizabeth was too intelligent and shrewd to be manipulated by Dudley. Dudley pointed out to Edward that his sisters still were technically illegitimate. As female rulers, they also might marry foreign princes who would swallow up England.

Dudley authorized doctors to treat Edward with the poison arsenic, agonizingly prolonging his life until, in great pain, Edward finally agreed to the change of succession. Because he was a minor, it was illegal for

Lady Jane Grey.

Edward to change his father's will, which had been confirmed by Parliament. Regardless, Edward named his sixteen-year-old Protestant cousin Lady Jane Grey heiress to the throne. Jane's power-hungry parents forced her to marry Guilford Dudley, the lord protector's son. As a reluctant political puppet, Jane disagreed with the council's plans. "The crown is not my right, and pleaseth me not," she said. "The Lady Mary is the rightful heir."

Edward died on July 6, 1553, and Jane was quickly crowned. Edward's advisors summoned Elizabeth and Mary to court, hoping to imprison the two sisters and prevent them from seizing the throne. Secretly, friends at court warned them not to come. Elizabeth stayed at Hatfield, nervously waiting for news.

Robert Dudley led a group of men to try to capture Mary. She managed to elude them, then quickly rounded up her troops and Catholic supporters. Mary also had the backing of many people who disliked the lord protector's

During her reign, Mary I returned England to Catholic rule. *(Prado Museum, Madrid)*

greed and disregard for the law. After only nine days, Jane Grey's reign was over. Mary Tudor was now queen of England.

Laying aside any differences, Elizabeth acted at once

to show her loyalty to Mary. She immediately wrote to congratulate her sister and prepared to join Mary's entourage. A few days later, Elizabeth rode into London with 2,000 horses and men clothed in green and white, the colors of the Tudor family. In advertising her family heritage, Elizabeth was supporting Mary and reminding all of England that she had the right to be queen some-day, too.

Elizabeth rode behind Mary in her coronation pa-rade. There was no hint that Elizabeth was out of favor with her sister, though the relationship between them had never been easy. Not only were their personalities different, but they had grown up in opposite circum-stances. Mary disputed Elizabeth's place in the succes-sion, believing her to be illegitimate because the Catho-lic Church had never recognized their father's divorce from Mary's mother, Catherine of Aragon. Mary wa-vered between bitterness at having been disinherited and sending Elizabeth necklaces and pocket money.

Religion ultimately poisoned the relationship be-tween the two sisters. Mary was determined to restore Catholicism to England and rejected advice that it would lead to more division. Northern and western England were primarily Catholic, but Protestantism had put down deep roots in London and the southeast. While most people were glad to see Mary, as the rightful heir, re-stored to the throne, not many were anxious to return to Catholicism.

When Elizabeth continued to quietly practice her

Protestant religion, Mary took it as a personal insult. She became increasingly hostile towards Elizabeth and put intense pressure on her to convert. Elizabeth couldn't risk angering Mary or appearing traitorous by not embracing Catholicism. Drawing on her acting skills, she tearfully begged Mary for instruction in religion, saying she had a defective upbringing. Softhearted Mary relented. Then, to avoid going to Mass, Elizabeth pretended to be sick, telling everyone her stomach hurt. Mary and her council eventually grew frustrated. "Everyone believes that she is acting rather from fear of danger and peril than from real devotion," said the French ambassador about Elizabeth's conversion to Catholicism.

Elizabeth was treading a fine line between encouraging her many Protestant supporters and staying in Queen Mary's good graces. Due to the mounting tension, Elizabeth asked to leave court in December of 1553. Knowing Mary would be quick to believe any rumors about her, Elizabeth begged her sister for the opportunity to defend herself in person, if ever the need arose. Ten miles out of London, she sent a messenger back to Mary to borrow chapel ornaments so she could follow the Catholic faith and observe Mass. It was a dramatic gesture intended to convince Mary of her innocence and trustworthiness. Mary wasn't fooled this time. She was convinced Elizabeth would "bring about some great evil unless she is dealt with."

In the meantime, Mary decided she needed a husband. Women were widely believed to be weak, and it would have been highly unusual for one to rule alone. Mary also wanted heirs. She set her sights on King Philip II of Spain.

When the Holy Roman Emperor Charles V abdicated his throne in the mid-1550s, he divided his empire, changing the face of Europe. His son Philip was given Spain, Naples and Milan in Italy, the Netherlands, and the Spanish empire in the Americas. Charles's brother, Ferdinand, succeeded him as emperor and held the crowns of Austria, Bohemia, and Hungary. The Holy Roman Empire was a patchwork of lands that Charles had barely managed to hold together. Now any sense of cohesion was lost. The divided empire continued to be threatened by the expansion of the Ottoman Empire, the rise of Protestantism, and its traditional French enemies.

The Protestants began to split into rival factions, including Lutherans, Calvinists, Anabaptists, Zwinglians, and others, and Europe became even more fragmented. Nations began to develop their own geographic and religious independence.

When Charles V abdicated, he moved to a monastery to spend the rest of his days in prayer and devotion. His son, now Philip II, inherited his father's dedication to Catholicism and was determined to stamp out Protestantism. Mary's decision to wed such a fiercely Catholic king upset Protestants, and the idea of a foreign king angered many in England, from Mary's aged councilors to the small boys on the street who pelted the Spanish ambassadors with snowballs. Religion was not the only

problem with the marriage. English people didn't generally trust foreigners, especially their long-standing
Spanish and French rivals. As the tension increased,
there was talk of revolt. Elizabeth, as Mary's heir, inevi-
tably became a magnet for treason.

Any conspiracy, even if Elizabeth did not condone it,
risked her life. All Mary needed was the slightest hint that
Elizabeth was scheming against her to have her sister
convicted of treason and put to death. Elizabeth took
pains to be careful of what she did, said, or put in writing.

"Bloody" Mary with her Catholic husband, Philip II of Spain. *(Woburn Abbey, Bedfordshire)*

Mary's wedding plans did put a treasonous plan in motion, led by Thomas Wyatt, Henry Grey (Lady Jane's father), and Edward Courtenay. The men planned a series of regional uprisings after which rebels would march on London to overthrow the government. Elizabeth would then marry Courtenay and become queen. But their scheme was discovered. In January 1554, Wyatt led his troops to London, but Mary's army was there and forced him to surrender. He was taken to the tower. As the news spread, people began to wonder how much Elizabeth had known about Wyatt's rebellion.

After Wyatt's arrest, Mary wrote to Elizabeth urging her to come to court for her own safety. Elizabeth, worried it was a trap, said she was ill and the country was too dangerous for travel. She asked for the queen's doctors to verify her excuse. Mary sent a posse to bring Elizabeth to court. Elizabeth pleaded she couldn't make the journey "without peril of her life," but the royal doctors said she was well enough to travel.

The journey should have taken five days, but Elizabeth, carried in a litter, bided her time. As she traveled toward London, word came that Queen Mary had executed Jane Grey, whom she had known since infancy. Fearing that she was being carried to her death at the hands of her sister, Elizabeth became very ill. She had pains in her arms and head. Her whole body was swollen, symptoms of kidney disease or illness brought on by stress.

After a ten-day trip, Elizabeth made a dramatic entry

This famous 1833 Paul Delaroche painting of Jane Grey's execution at the Tower of London has helped to popularize the tragic story of the young Protestant queen. *(National Portrait Gallery, London)*

into the city. The pale princess, visibly ill, flung back the curtains to her litter so all of London could see her. Dressed in white, the symbol of innocence, Elizabeth wanted to show everyone her sister was forcing her to come to court. Then, for three weeks, Elizabeth lay in the palace, sick and alone, with no word from Mary.

Meanwhile, Mary's investigation uncovered scraps of evidence indicating the conspirators had kept Elizabeth informed of their plans. Wyatt had written to Elizabeth, urging her to move to a safer house. There was no proof, however, that Elizabeth had condoned their actions.

Mary's council urged Elizabeth to throw herself at the queen's mercy and beg for a pardon. Elizabeth knew this would be tantamount to confessing to the crime. Instead, she steadfastly denied any knowledge of the conspirators' plans. None of the men arrested implicated her, even under torture. Before Wyatt was beheaded, boiled, and quartered, he shouted from the scaffold that Elizabeth had no knowledge of the uprising.

On March 17, two days after Wyatt's execution, Mary's councilors arrived to escort Elizabeth to the Tower of London by boat. Elizabeth feared she would be executed without being able to speak to her sister first. She begged to be allowed to write Mary a letter. The councilors relented. Elizabeth sat down and wrote, slowly and carefully, pleading for her life and swearing her innocence.

"If anyone ever did try this old saying," Elizabeth wrote, "'that a king's word was more than another man's oath,' I most humbly beseech your majesty to verify it to me, and to remember your last promise and my last demand—that I not be condemned without answer and due proof." Elizabeth's letter filled one page and part of a second. She covered the rest of the page with long, diagonal lines, so no one could forge anything under her signature. As Elizabeth wrote, the tide turned on the river. Now the trip couldn't be made safely. Elizabeth had bought herself a few hours, but it was not enough. Mary refused to read the letter.

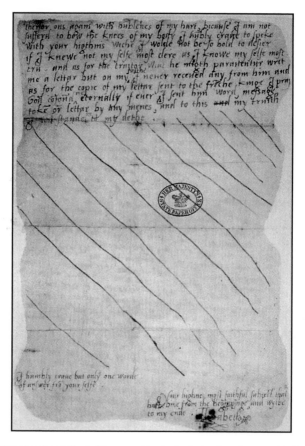

Elizabeth's pleading letter to Mary, sent just prior to her imprisonment in the Tower of London. *(National Archives, Surrey)*

The next morning Elizabeth was imprisoned in the tower. She spent every day overlooking the green lawn where her mother had died, wondering when her own death might come. Candles and smoky torches lit her circular room. Personal servants cooked her food to make sure it wasn't poisoned. It was soon obvious that the evidence wasn't strong enough to have her executed. Even though Mary wanted her sister out of the way, she had to accept that sentencing Elizabeth to death would anger the English people and make enemies of many powerful councilors she could not afford to alienate. After two nerve-racking months of imprisonment, Elizabeth was sent to live under house arrest at Mary's damp and crumbling manor of Woodstock.

As Elizabeth traveled through London, people cheered, thinking she was free. She journeyed north to the leaky, cramped rooms at Woodstock to be watched over by Sir Henry Bedingfield, her Catholic jailor. Along the route, men, women, and children gathered to watch her pass. They piled her litter with flowers, cakes, meat pies, and other small gifts. From the streets of London to the rural countryside, citizens flocked to Elizabeth. The power of the English people was behind her.

As Mary's new husband, Philip, entered England with 9,000 noblemen and servants, and twenty carts carrying ninety-seven treasure chests, Elizabeth was busy bedeviling her guards. She managed to smuggle in forbidden books, even though everything but her underwear was searched. With a diamond, she scratched on a windowpane, "Much suspected, by me. Nothing proved can be, Quoth Elizabeth, Prisoner." But Mary wasn't concerned with Elizabeth any longer. She was married and soon expecting a child—who would become the next heir to the throne.

In April 1555, Elizabeth was commanded back to court to be present for the birth of Mary's child. Elizabeth knelt at the queen's feet, praying for her sister's health and begging Mary to believe her innocence.

Although Mary was doubtful, Philip pressured her to make amends with Elizabeth. Mary's husband, unpopular in England, wanted Elizabeth's support and protection if Mary died during childbirth. He had lost his first wife that way and knew the danger was real. Before the discovery of antibiotics, any infection could be fatal.

One week later, Elizabeth was free from guards and house arrest. Now she waited, along with all of England, for Mary's delivery. Months passed and no baby was born. Mary was experiencing what today is called pseudocyesis, or false pregnancy, a condition in which a woman's desire for a child prompts her body to mimic the symptoms of pregnancy. Bitter, Philip left England without any definite plans to return. Mary was devastated, and her government suffered.

The crowds of people, who so jubilantly welcomed Mary to the throne, were turning against her. She was nicknamed "Bloody Mary" for instituting mass executions in which over three hundred Protestants were burned alive for refusing to practice Catholicism. Instead of reinstating her beloved religion, Mary's actions incited nationwide hatred of her and the Catholic religion. Mary had let Philip talk her into joining Spain in a costly war against France over disputed territories. It had not gone well. The port city of Calais, held by England since the fourteenth century, had been lost to France. Mary was blamed for everything from poor crops to chilly summer weather.

The suffering citizens of England began to look to

Elizabeth for hope—the wily Philip included. He wanted to ensure Elizabeth would support Spain if she succeeded Mary. He and Mary tried to wed her to a Spanish general, but Elizabeth's position was now too strong to be pressured into a marriage to satisfy Spain's needs.

In August 1558, shortly after experiencing a second false pregnancy, Mary fell ill with influenza. By October, she was dying. Philip pushed Mary to officially name Elizabeth as her successor. Mary did, on the condition that Elizabeth would uphold the Catholic faith. Elizabeth swore she would but had no intention to fulfill the promise. Nobody but Mary believed she would.

In the weeks before Mary's death, the entire country committed themselves to Elizabeth. The roads to Hatfield were thronged with courtiers coming to pledge their allegiance. By November, there was a holiday-like atmosphere at Hatfield. Elizabeth was receiving volumes of mail and visitors daily. On November 17, Queen Mary died.

Londoners closed shops and markets in celebration. They lit bonfires on every street corner, and ate and drank, toasting Elizabeth far into the night.

It was a quieter scene at Hatfield. Elizabeth was reading under an oak tree when she was told of Mary's death. It was noon on a cold autumn day. She sank to her knees, speechless for a few minutes. Then she said, in Latin, *"A Domine factum est illud et est mirabile in oculis nostris!"* (This is the doing of the Lord; and it is marvelous in our eyes!) The reign of Queen Elizabeth I had begun.

A KINGDOM IN SHAMBLES

Elizabeth's coronation was set for January 15, 1559. The day before, she would progress through London to the tower, where tradition held that royalty spend the night before being crowned. Though Elizabeth had unhappy memories of that place, she was determined to make this coronation one to remember. The entire kingdom was set in motion. Day and night, people prepared for feasts, plays, dances, and parades. While Elizabeth's golden gown was a hand-me-down from Mary, tailored to fit her, every one of her servants and advisors had new clothes for the occasion.

For several days there had been steady drizzle. At the best of times, England's narrow roads were challenging. Most were mere footpaths, all but impassable in the winter. Now the streets of London were muddy and

Created by a German mapmaker in the year before Elizabeth's coronation, this map gives a good sense of the tightly knotted maze of streets that made up central London during Tudor reign. *(Courtesy of the Granger Collection.)*

slushy. Workmen filled the deepest puddles and holes along the parade route with gravel.

At three o'clock in the afternoon on the eve of her coronation, Elizabeth began the slow parade to the tower. As snowflakes fell from the gray winter sky, Londoners cheered for their new queen. She was followed by one thousand horses and a procession of attendants and noblemen, in colorful satins and velvets, that took an hour to pass. Throughout London, people performed pageants to entertain her. They threw bouquets of flowers and herbs as she passed by in her golden litter. Elizabeth was determined to impress everyone with her magnificence and wealth, showing the entire world she was the rightful queen. The festivities cost nearly 17,000 pounds, more than a merchant family might earn in four generations.

Everywhere along her route, Elizabeth stopped and listened to people. She answered their good wishes with kind words of her own. "God save your grace!" they called. "God save you all!" she shouted back, adding, "I thank you with all of my heart." Queen Mary had been shy and quiet in crowds. Elizabeth made people feel as though she was as grateful for their small bouquets as she was for the purse of gold given to her when she entered London. The people loved her and she loved them in return.

"If ever any person had either the gift or the style to win the hearts of the people, it was this queen," said one of her subjects.

The following day, Elizabeth was officially crowned queen of England. She was dressed all in gold, from her golden shoes to her weighty golden crown. Her long red hair hung around her shoulders. To the sound of ringing trumpets, Elizabeth placed the coronation ring on the fourth finger of her right hand, symbolizing her marriage to the people of England.

As souvenir hunters cut up the seven hundred yards of blue carpet she walked in on, Elizabeth moved to the coronation banquet. Thousands along the way pressed up to offer their congratulations. The celebrations continued until one o'clock in the morning.

In this painting, known as the *Coronation Portrait,* Elizabeth is dressed much like a bride, in a gold-and-ermine gown with her long hair flowing over her shoulders. She holds the ruler's orb and scepter as a symbol of her power. *(National Portrait Gallery, London)*

After the festivities were over, Elizabeth got to work. She had inherited serious problems, many of which needed immediate attention. "The burden that has fallen upon me maketh me amazed," she said.

Elizabeth's England was an agricultural economy. About three-quarters of the population lived in the

Townspeople in coastal Yarmouth, a typical sixteenth-century town, made their living from the nearby fields and grazing lands, as well as fishing. *(British Library, London)*

countryside, where nearly 650 towns and 10,000 small villages dotted the land. Transportation was expensive, exhausting, and dangerous. London and Paris were a two-day journey apart. During the winter, letters might take months to get through.

English society was divided into an upper class of nobles, knights, and gentlemen; a middle class of merchants and businessmen; and a lower class of craftsmen and farmers. In typical families, men worked as farmers or tradesmen, while women ran the households, managing children, servants, and apprentices. Most families had three to five children, while wealthier families had as many as twelve. Infant mortality rates were high, and even those who survived infancy were susceptible to diseases. When children reached their teens, they went to work as servants, farm hands, or apprentices.

Rural life centered on work from Monday through Saturday. Sundays were for rest and worship. For fun, people attended local church festivals and swapped stories at the local alehouse. They celebrated by feasting, dancing, watching plays, attending parties, and playing games and sports.

Lives were controlled by nature. Each season, people watched anxiously as rain or sun shaped their lives into a season of famine or a season of plenty. Disease also wreaked havoc. Bubonic plague, or the Black Death, raged during hot summer months. Overcrowded towns and poor sanitation helped air and waterborne infections run rampant. Believing baths to be dangerous to their health, most people took them only twice a year. The average life expectancy was forty years.

Industry, such as textiles and mining, had begun to sprout in various parts of the country. But it was held back by the inadequate and antiquated monetary system. A variety of coins circulated—pennies, groats, shillings, farthings, crowns, sovereigns, and angels. The pound, £, represented the weight or sum of the money. An unskilled laborer might earn £7 in a year.

England shared its island with the countries Wales and Scotland, and was near the island of Ireland. Gradually, the English had come to dominate both islands. Under Henry VIII, English customs had begun to replace the Welsh traditions. King Henry II had invaded Ireland in 1170, and there had been several clashes since. In 1541, Henry VIII had declared himself king of Ireland,

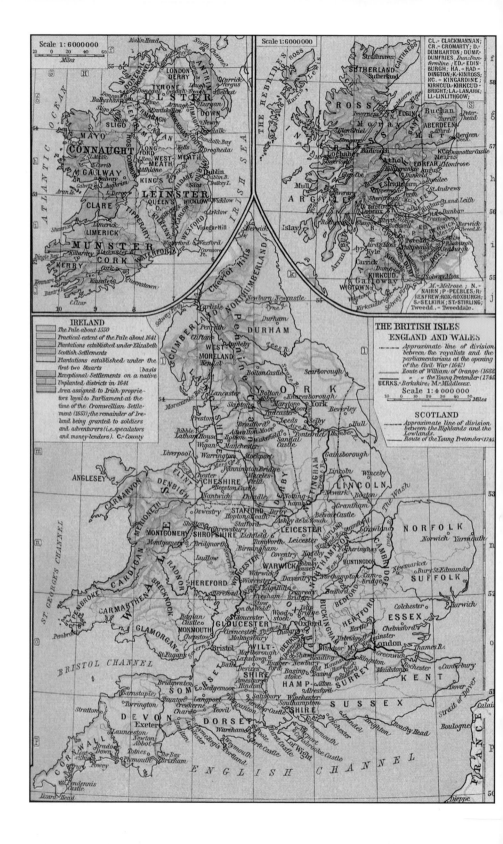

Scale 1:6000000
20 0 20 40 60
Miles

Scale 1:6000000

IRELAND
The Pale about 1550
Practical extent of the Pale about 1641
Plantations established under Elizabeth
Scottish Settlements
Plantations established under the
first two Stuarts [basis
Exceptional Settlements on a native
Unplanted districts in 1641
Area assigned to Irish proprie-
tors loyal to Parliament at the
time of the Cromwellian Settle-
ment (1653); the remainder of Ire-
land being granted to soldiers
and adventurers (i.e.speculators
and money-lenders). C.= County

THE BRITISH ISLES
ENGLAND AND WALES
        Approximate line of division
        between the royalists and the
        parliamentarians at the opening
        of the Civil War (1642)
        Route of William of Orange (1688
    "   " the Young Pretender (1745
BERKS.= Berkshire; M.= Middlesex.
Scale 1:4000000
20 0 10 20 30 40 50 Miles

SCOTLAND
        Approximate line of division
        between the Highlands and the
        Lowlands.
        Route of the Young Pretender 1745

but the English still struggled to create an Irish state that recognized only English law and custom. One source of conflict in the sixteenth century was that most Irish were still Catholic. England had also long had designs on Scotland, which still had its own rulers and was at the time allied with France.

While there continued to be conflicts between Catholic countries, France and Spain remained enemies. France aligned itself squarely against the predominantly Catholic Holy Roman Empire, and within France the Catholic ruling family, the Valois, was pitted against Protestant nobles. Much of central Europe was wracked by sectarian conflict, most of which took place within countries as one group attempted to dominate, or eliminate, another.

The problem of religion became entangled with foreign policy when Catholic or Protestant monarchs came to the aid of their co-religionists in other lands. By the middle of the century, the European political situation was a confusing pattern of shifting alliances and deceit determined by overlapping religious, territorial, and economic concerns. It was a treacherous time to be a ruler.

At the same time, the fifteenth-century discovery of new lands in America and trade routes to Asia and the Middle East changed international trade and exploration. Europe was beginning to look westward, across the Atlantic Ocean, in search of new wealth. England, as an island on the western edge of Europe, was well placed

Opposite: The British Isles in the sixteenth century.

to participate in the rush to settle and claim large sections of the Americas. It would be necessary to build a military and merchant navy large enough to take advantage of the new opportunities.

Young Queen Elizabeth had to find a way to deal with these multifaceted and interconnected problems and opportunities. It sometimes seemed overwhelming. One courtier listed the litany of problems she faced: "The Queen poor, the realm exhausted, the nobility poor and decayed. Want of good captains and soldiers. The people out of order. Justice not executed. All things dear [costly]. Excess in meat, drink, apparel. Divisions among ourselves. Wars with France and Scotland. The French king bestriding our realm, having one foot in Calais and the other in Scotland. Steadfast enmity but no steadfast friendship abroad."

Three problems needed immediate attention. The first was the threat of invasion. Philip and Mary's war against France had created an alliance between France and Scotland. Enemies surrounded Elizabeth's realm. Second, Elizabeth needed to avert a religious civil war within England. The third problem was financial. The country and the crown were broke.

Many people doubted Elizabeth's ability to solve the country's problems. Mary had justified long-held doubts about women rulers. Women were assumed to be weak, impatient, and foolish. They should keep silent around men and obey their husbands and fathers. Though many women didn't always observe these rules of society, few openly flaunted them. But Elizabeth, the daughter of Henry VIII, saw herself as a sovereign appointed by God and believed her gender was irrelevant: "My sex cannot diminish my prestige," she said.

Though Elizabeth had been living outside of London at Hatfield, her contacts at court had kept her well informed. She knew the issues and the personalities she would have to deal with as queen. And her life experiences had taught her how to keep her mouth shut and her eyes and ears open.

Immediately after Mary's death, Elizabeth began to choose her council and servants. Each monarch shaped his or her own council, which consisted of men of influence and business experience, along with the ruler's personal servants. Henry VIII's secretary, Thomas Cromwell, had created a tight inner circle of advisors called the Privy Council that contained the monarch's most important advisors: chancellor, treasurer, and secretary of state. The Privy Council met daily, formulating and executing the royal policies. It was "the eyes, ears, and the tongue of the Prince and the realm."

Elizabeth named William Cecil her secretary of state. Cecil had been her faithful servant since 1550. Intelligent and ambitious, Cecil also had served under Mary. Although he had been discreet in his Protestantism during her reign, he sadly recorded in his journal the name of every Protestant executed for heresy. As secretary of state, Cecil was responsible for the government's foreign policy and secret service. He created the agenda

Elizabeth's lifelong councilor, William Cecil.

for council meetings and relayed the details of the meetings to Elizabeth if she were absent. Elizabeth knew Cecil would give her good advice. She nicknamed him "Spirit," as she often gave pet names to people she liked.

Next, Elizabeth remodeled the council. She dismissed two-thirds of Mary's councilors, keeping the remaining ten men to ensure a smooth transition. She then added appointees of her own. Some were high-ranking aristocrats with vast political experience. The rest were noblemen, lawyers, and businessmen chosen for their intelligence rather than their status in society.

Elizabeth also rewarded friends for past loyalty, giving some of her mother's relatives positions at court. Kat Ashley became first lady of the bedchamber, a much-honored position. Robert Dudley was made master of the horse, responsible for maintaining and buying horses for the queen's stables.

Choosing the right servants was critical to the queen's

safety. Servants close to her, attending her physical and emotional needs, could easily do her harm if they were bribed or disloyal. Elizabeth's chamber ladies dished out her food and could easily poison her. Elizabeth wisely dismissed all of Mary's personal friends, replacing them with her own. Surrounding herself with this circle of trusted old friends and relatives protected her and made her comfortable.

During her childhood, Elizabeth had learned many of the skills she needed to be a good queen. She knew how to be evasive—even deceitful—and how to conceal her goals. She had learned to suppress her emotions and to shrewdly calculate each move.

Elizabeth took an intense interest in her government and country. She worked hard every day. She attended the Privy Council's meetings and didn't embroider handkerchiefs to pass the time as the queen of Scotland was said to do. Her tenacity earned her the respect of Parliament and council.

Elizabeth's Parliament was made up of two houses. The lower house, or House of Commons, had 310 members. There were two representatives from every county and important town. The upper house, or House of Lords, had 107 members. The House of Lords was composed of the leading clergy and noblemen. The queen had great power over Parliament. Elizabeth could call Parliament and dissolve it at her will. She could adjourn sessions and veto bills. Elizabeth was not required by law to share policy making with Parliament, but its approval was

Elizabeth, in plain yet elegant dress, during the early years of her reign.

needed for new laws.

Elizabeth often met with her councilors individually to keep them from uniting against her. She sometimes played upon their feelings and controlled them by being unpredictable, using a mixture of temper and humor to manipulate them. Elizabeth acted like a queen from the start, stating her wishes and then leaving the room so there could be no argument. Men were not used to obeying orders given by a woman. The new Spanish ambassador, the Count of Feria, was completely bewildered. Elizabeth was a strange sort of woman, he wrote to Philip II. She was "more feared than her sister, and gives her orders and has her way as absolutely as her father did."

Elizabeth's childhood and teenage years had made her a master at the art of deception. She kept everyone guessing as to her intentions, often exasperating her councilors and servants. Often Elizabeth delayed giving answers, or gave one answer and then changed her mind. She was adept at playing two sides in a conflict against each other. This tactic helped prevent plots against her and allowed her to hear both sides of an argument. By waiting for conflicts to unfold and by not making rash decisions, Elizabeth avoided many problems. But the three emergencies she inherited from the start could not wait.

Elizabeth needed to disengage her country from war with powerful France. In Mary's final hours, important papers negotiating the treaty between England and France had been brought to her to sign. Too weak, Mary had left the papers beside her bed until she died. Now they were nowhere to be found. Mary's waiting woman informed Elizabeth that the embalmers had found the long rolls of parchment useful for wrapping Mary's corpse. Peace talks stalled while copies were made of the documents.

Peace with France involved the difficult problem of Scotland. James V of Scotland had died unexpectedly in 1542. In the years following, Henry VIII had led a military campaign against Scotland because of its alliance with Catholic France. James's young daughter, Mary Queen of Scots, had been sent to France to marry the heir to the French throne. French troops safeguarded Mary's mother, who ruled Scotland until her daughter could return. France encouraged Scotland to continue to be a thorn in the side of England, its longtime enemy.

Mary Queen of Scots was Elizabeth's cousin, the granddaughter of Henry VIII's oldest sister Margaret.

When Henry created his will, he was at war with Scotland and had ↙passed Margaret's descendants in favor of his younger sister's heirs. Many people, especially Catholics, believed that Mary had a strong claim to the throne of England. With France's backing, Mary presented a very real threat to Elizabeth.

Elizabeth needed to find a way to make peace with France, but she did not want to abandon English claims to the city of Calais on the French coast. Luckily, she had a negotiating trick up her sleeve. Her Spanish brother-in-law, Philip II, had proposed marriage to her. Elizabeth hoped to intimidate France by advertising the fact that powerful, wealthy Spain was in her corner—at least until the peace talks were finished. The ploy worked. In early April 1559, peace was finally reached between England and France, and France and Spain, with the signing of the Treaty of Cateau-Cambrésis. The port city of Calais would remain in French hands for eight years, after which Elizabeth hoped to recover it. Most importantly, England was no longer at war.

Now Elizabeth no longer needed to pretend that she wanted to marry Philip. She politely refused his marriage proposal, citing their religious differences. Philip wanted Elizabeth to uphold the Catholic faith, and she was innately Protestant. Philip was not overly disappointed. He would have liked to add England to his possessions, but he knew Elizabeth had strong opinions that were very different from his. Philip quickly married a thirteen-year-old French princess.

Now Elizabeth turned her attentions to the religious divisions between Protestants and Catholics. Although people had their own personal beliefs, in the sixteenth century religious practice was not seen as a purely private matter. Each country in Europe had a state religion, enforced by law.

Edward had continued moving England toward Protestantism. Then Queen Mary had returned the nation to Catholicism. During her reign, nearly eight hundred English Protestants fled, fearing persecution. Those left were a small, but vocal, minority. They looked to Elizabeth as their savior, hoping she would further advance the Reformation.

Protestant Elizabeth feared the power of English Catholics. Confronting their position was dangerous. Furthermore, Elizabeth disliked extremists on both sides. Her ultimate concerns were political rather than religious. She wanted a settlement between the two groups that would unite as many of her subjects as possible.

On April 29, 1559, after much debate, Elizabeth's Parliament passed the Act of Supremacy and the Act of Uniformity. The Act of Supremacy created Elizabeth as the supreme governor of the Church of England. The Act of Uniformity set up approved forms of worship and changed text in the Book of Common Prayer, which Edward had introduced, so that it appealed to both Catholic and Protestant beliefs. The book was written and services were conducted in English rather than Latin, but kept some of the elements of Catholic rituals, including the use of candles and crucifixes and elaborate dress for the clergy. Other Catholic practices, such as the belief in miracles and the sale of indulgences, or payments to priests, were abandoned. Attending church services was mandatory and there were small fines—usually not enforced—for violators. Although England was officially a Protestant country, Catholics were not punished for practicing their faith in private.

Elizabeth remembered her difficulties with religion during Mary's reign, along with her months in the Tower of London. Not making emotional decisions was important to Elizabeth. As long as people who remained Catholic at heart were loyal to her, Elizabeth had no desire to punish them. Her tolerance helped ease the religious tension England had experienced since the 1530s. Religious agendas, however, would continue to shape domestic affairs and foreign relations, and would continue to plague her country long after her death.

The third crisis requiring Elizabeth's immediate attention was financial. Past rulers had debased the English currency, reducing the amount of silver in the coins from 90 percent to 25 percent. The money was now worth less than its face value. Foreign merchants refused to accept the coins, requiring English buyers to pay them in pure gold, leading to a shortage of gold. Past attempts to collect all of the debased coins had failed. In 1560, Elizabeth and Cecil created a program to revalue the money. Elizabeth guaranteed if people brought their debased coins to the mint, they could exchange them for newly minted coins worth the same amount. London goldsmiths melted down old coins and used the pure metal inside to create the new coins. Nearly £700,000 of debased currency was returned to the mint and refined. This complex undertaking solved a problem plaguing England for years.

The first year of Elizabeth's reign was successful. She ruled with tolerance yet firmness, a style her subjects were yearning for after the years of turmoil under her Tudor relatives. The people loved their new queen, and she showered them with affection. But many wondered how long it would be until her thoughts turned to marriage. Strength and governing was a man's job. Surely, Elizabeth would be married soon.

4

LOVE AND POLITICS

In the warm summer of 1559, Elizabeth had a brief respite from the tensions of governing. For a week she entertained a group of French ambassadors who came to ratify the new peace treaty. At the palace of Whitehall, along the Thames River, she led hunting parties in the park and hosted magnificent outdoor banquets. One feast took place in the palace gardens, the tables surrounded by gold and silver hangings and sweet-smelling wreaths made from flowers and leaves.

The summer continued with singing, dancing, and evening trips on the royal barge. Everyone hoped Elizabeth's thoughts would soon turn to romance. She was twenty-five years old, a sixteenth-century spinster. The kingdom and the rest of Europe wondered when and to whom she would get married.

Elizabeth and her courtiers enjoy the outdoors during one of the lavish picnics the queen commanded throughout her reign.

"The Queen is of an age where she should in reason, and as is woman's way, be eager to marry and be provided for. . . . For that she should wish to remain a maid and never marry is inconceivable," said a German diplomat. Elizabeth held a position that was seen as being beyond a woman's capabilities. Everyone believed her female mind needed a man's assistance to help her govern so she could be "relieved of the pains and travails which were rather men's work than the profession of ladies," according to Philip II.

Marriage offered Elizabeth and England certain benefits. Although royal marriages were not usually love matches, she would have a partner whom she might grow to love. Marriage also presented the opportunity to form an alliance. The royal couple could have children who would inherit the throne, guaranteeing the smooth succession of England's next ruler.

Finding an acceptable husband for Elizabeth posed problems for her and her realm. The man she married would become king of England. Men young and old, from England and abroad, craved this power. Despite the advantages of forging a foreign alliance, England did not want to be ruled by a foreign prince—and neither did Elizabeth. She remembered how Mary had lost favor when she married the king of Spain. Although Spain had provided protection from France, Elizabeth knew marrying a foreigner could undermine her authority.

If Elizabeth didn't marry a foreign prince, then her options were limited to marrying a man from within her own kingdom. This too was problematic. Many factions at court were vying for her favor. Supporting one man above the others could lead to civil war. Elizabeth also couldn't marry someone beneath her in social status.

Some of Elizabeth's biggest assets were that she was an attractive, unmarried queen, loved by her country and her court. Her own thoughts about marriage, shaped by the events in her childhood, were not positive. Seventeen years earlier, after her father executed a second wife, Elizabeth had sworn she would never marry. There was another reason to avoid taking a husband. Marriage meant children, and Elizabeth feared childbirth. About one out of one hundred women died from childbirth in the sixteenth century, and even more in London. Elizabeth's grandmother and two of her stepmothers had died from childbirth. Elizabeth had also witnessed her sister's humiliating phantom pregnancies. Elizabeth was determined to stay single.

When Elizabeth's Parliament questioned her about marrying, Elizabeth said she would be content to have engraved on her tombstone, "that a Queen, having reigned such a time, lived and died a virgin." This was such a startling idea that few in her government believed her. That suited Elizabeth quite well. Sometimes, though, the pressure cracked even her famous composure. When Elizabeth's Privy Council pressed her to get married, she flashed her coronation ring and said firmly, "I am already bound unto a husband, which is the kingdom of England. Every one of you, and as many as are Englishmen, are children and kinsmen to me."

Despite her protestations, Elizabeth did not lack for suitors. Prince Erik of Sweden wrote love letters in Latin. Ivan the Terrible of Russia threw in his hand, as did Archduke Ferdinand of Austria and his brother Charles. The dukes of Saxony and Holstein also added themselves to the list of suitors.

Elizabeth strung her suitors along, dangling the promise of marriage and playing them like pieces on a chessboard. This went on for years, as Elizabeth claimed to be seriously trying to choose a husband. The longer she kept up the possibility of a marriage between two countries, the longer relations between those countries were favorable and helpful. She became highly adept at stalling tactics, often inventing difficulties to a marriage to delay giving definite answers. Her council was horrified that she actually seemed to consider some of the suitors placed before her. "Princes . . . transact business in a certain way, with a princely intelligence, such as private persons cannot imitate," was her lofty response to their concerns.

Usually it was an ambassador who proposed marriage to Elizabeth, rather than the prince himself. Foreign princes worried that if they presented themselves to Elizabeth and she refused them, the rejection would dishonor them and their countries. Elizabeth used this to her advantage, repeatedly stating that she could not marry a man she had never seen. She knew very well it was not unusual for a couple to meet face to face for the first time at their wedding ceremony, but she pretended to abhor the idea so as to buy more time in the negotiations, keeping the countries involved in a state of forced friendliness.

In August 1559, a group of influential Scottish Protestant nobles asked for Elizabeth's help. They were tired of the French influence in their country and wanted to advance their religion over the French-sponsored Catholicism. Cecil suggested they offer English support of the Scottish rebels, as long as Mary Queen of Scots remained in France. They did not want Mary's claim to the throne threatening her from the north. Mary and her husband Francis II had recently been crowned king and queen of France.

Although she wanted to support the Protestants in Scotland, Elizabeth hesitated to risk war with France. She sent Cecil to Edinburgh to try to negotiate with the Scots and French. Soon after he arrived, two things happened: Mary's mother died, which left Mary in line for the throne, and religious civil war broke out in France.

The French Protestants, called Huguenots, had been increasing in political influence. To counteract their power, the Catholic League, a union of nobles and church-men led by the Guise family, relatives of Mary Queen of Scots, was organized to militantly champion the Catholic cause. France soon erupted into some of the most terrible religious violence in Europe. The once proud and wealthy country would be weakened by reli-gious civil wars for the next thirty years.

Unable to risk war with England over Scotland, France agreed to the Treaty of Edinburgh in July of 1560. It withdrew all but a token French force from Scotland, where James Stuart, who was the Earl of Moray and Mary's half brother, set up a Protestant government.

Elizabeth had achieved her objectives. War with France had been avoided and she had taken a bold step by becoming a protector to foreign Protestant commu-nities. But this success made it even more difficult to maintain good relations with Catholic monarchs.

Elizabeth had been pushed by her councilors to make certain decisions during the Scottish affair. Although the problem had been solved to England's advantage, Elizabeth was determined that from then on, she would not allow herself to be dependent on one advisor or group of advisors. As a strong female ruler, she needed to show she could master men and events.

Yet one man threatened to be her undoing. The worst-kept secret in England was that Queen Elizabeth was in love. Not with a foreign prince but with her friend, the tall, athletic Robert Dudley. The two had known each other since they played together as children. Dudley also had been imprisoned in the Tower of London after Wyatt's rebellion. To Elizabeth, Dudley was a cultured, intelligent, and witty companion. She could be herself with him as with few other people. Elizabeth nicknamed him "Robin" and "Eyes," as he became her helpful informant, and showered him with gifts. He was already the honored master of the horse, running Elizabeth's royal stables. She gave him Kenilworth Castle and the license to a sweet wines farm, which brought him nearly £2,500 a year. She also gave him a yearly pension of £1,000. Dudley was now enormously wealthy.

Elizabeth and Dudley were inseparable, hunting and riding during the day, and playing card games and talking late into the night. Tongues flew as Dudley's status and wealth rose. Many disliked him out of envy, but Dudley also had a reputation for being ambitious

Elizabeth and Dudley dance a galliard, a lively sixteenth-century dance that was purported to be Elizabeth's favorite. *(National Portrait Gallery, London)*

and arrogant. People remembered his brother, father, and grandfather had been executed for treason under previous rulers. They wondered whether he loved Elizabeth or was using her to gain wealth and influence.

Elizabeth baffled everyone. The Spanish ambassador wrote to Philip, "To say the truth I could not tell your majesty what this woman means to do with herself, and those that know her best know no more than I do." Kat Ashley begged Elizabeth to be careful and to find a match that would be more pleasing to her subjects. Dudley had been married to Amy Robsart since 1551. Although they had no children and Amy lived in the country, never visiting court, Dudley was not free to marry as long as his wife was alive.

Though most of her subjects were enthralled by the queen, few would turn a blind eye to inappropriate behavior. Gossips buzzed. One rumor claimed Elizabeth and Dudley were married, another she was pregnant, and another they were plotting his wife's murder. Small details fanned the flames. Elizabeth once kissed Dudley on the lips; he took her handkerchief to wipe his face after playing tennis. Mutterings of plots to poison them both were heard at court. Cecil warned Elizabeth not to accept any gifts of perfume, gloves, or underclothes that could be tainted with poisons that could be absorbed through the skin. Tasters sampled all of Elizabeth's food.

The scandal began to endanger Elizabeth's chances of marrying abroad. It was acceptable for a man to have an affair, but not for a woman—especially a queen.

Then, Elizabeth's chance to marry the man she loved became possible and impossible at the same moment. On September 8, 1560, Dudley's wife was found dead at the bottom of a flight of stone steps. Her neck was broken, but her headdress was still neatly in place.

Amy Dudley had been dying of breast cancer. Her bones were brittle and she was weak. But whether she tripped and fell down the stairs or was murdered, no one knew. Dudley was banished from court until the scandal died down. Elizabeth tried to distance herself from him by demanding that an inquiry be made into Amy Dudley's death.

Mary Queen of Scots voiced a common sentiment

when she sniffed, "The Queen of England is going to marry her horsekeeper who has killed his wife to make room for her." Although Dudley was eventually found innocent, people still suspected him of plotting his wife's murder. Elizabeth, who appeared to have been truly tempted, could never marry Dudley now. Once the scandal died down, Dudley could remain her favorite, but she would not face pressure from him to marry. "I will have here but one mistress and no master," she announced.

Eventually, Dudley returned to Elizabeth's side. She appointed him to her council and soon afterwards made him the Earl of Leicester. During the ceremony, she could not resist reaching down and tickling him on the neck.

Despite the Dudley affair, Elizabeth's councilors continued to beg the twenty-nine-year-old queen to marry. If she died suddenly, without naming her successor, England could be thrown into chaos. Mary Queen of Scots might force her claim to the throne, bringing her Catholicism with her. Elizabeth's cousins, Katherine and Mary Grey, Jane's sisters, also had ties to the throne. Their grandmother was Henry VIII's sister. Following Henry's will, they were Elizabeth's heirs. But Elizabeth and many others disliked the Grey sisters. People argued that when their father had been convicted of treason for crowning Jane, his family forfeited their right to the throne. Another weaker claimant was Henry Hastings, a descendant of the medieval King Edward III.

Elizabeth remembered the plotting that had swirled

around her when she was the heir to the throne. She did not want to return to those days of uncertainty and fear. She avoided naming her successor because she feared doing so might motivate her enemies to try to work to unseat her. She did her best to assuage her council's concerns, but then the question of succession was soon brought to a crisis point.

On October 10, 1562, as Elizabeth took her daily walk in the gardens of Hampton Court Palace, she began to feel ill. She returned to her chambers and took a long bath, but only felt worse and soon went to bed with a high fever. Her servants summoned a doctor who diagnosed her with the dreaded, potentially fatal, smallpox. Those who survived were often left scarred from the pockmarks. In the 1560s, smallpox had reached epidemic proportions and had recently caused the death of one of Elizabeth's privy councilors.

By October 16, Elizabeth was unable to speak. As she drifted in and out of consciousness, her councilors met to decide upon a successor. They gathered around her bedchamber and discussed their options in hushed voices. Dudley summoned an army to the palace to head off any attackers who might try to usurp the throne. The entire kingdom waited. "Last night the people were all in mourning for her, as if she was already dead," said the Spanish ambassador.

After three days and nights, Elizabeth regained consciousness. Believing she was dying and about to face God's judgment, the sick queen dictated her will. Eliza-

Elizabeth's attachment to Robert Dudley began in childhood and continued throughout her life. (*The Wallace Collection, London*)

beth named Dudley lord protector, giving him a salary of £20,000 a year. She worried people would challenge Dudley's new position, thinking he was named lord protector because they had an affair. Elizabeth swore she loved Dudley but nothing improper had ever happened between them.

The doctor was summoned again. He wrapped Elizabeth in red cloth, leaving only her face and one hand exposed, and moved her close to the fire. Although the popular red treatment was an improbable cure for smallpox, it worked. Soon a stinging rash of pocks began to break out all over Elizabeth. With this, everyone breathed a sigh of relief. The danger of death was past. Elizabeth slowly recovered, although many worried she would be scarred for life. Remarkably, her skin stayed as pale and clear as it had been before the disease.

Elizabeth had returned from the brink of death. While some members of her council redoubled their efforts to find her a husband, others began to contemplate what the consequences might be if Elizabeth never married. They weighed the precarious religious balance of power in Europe and factored in Elizabeth's intelligence and shrewd diplomatic skills. Some began to see the benefit in England uniting behind its single, all-powerful queen.

On the morning Elizabeth became ill with smallpox, she had made an important decision. Dudley and Sir Nicholas Throckmorton, Elizabeth's French ambassador, had urged her to offer support to the Huguenots fighting in France. After much debate, she decided to send monetary aid and 6,000 soldiers, led by Dudley's brother, Ambrose. If she didn't send support, the Catholic monarchy would remain in power and might seek to oust her, possibly with Catholic Spain's help. Elizabeth also wanted the Huguenots to help reclaim the French port city of Calais.

In March 1563, the religious conflict in France had temporarily ended with the capture of the Huguenot leaders. Elizabeth still wanted her troops to fight for Calais, but the French forces, both Catholic and Protestant, now united against the English. They laid siege to Newhaven, the city in northern France occupied by the English troops. Months went by and the siege continued.

An epidemic of the plague swept through the city, decimating the English soldiers. As the plague-ridden army dwindled, hopes of regaining Calais also died. In July, Elizabeth finally allowed Ambrose Dudley to surrender.

As the soldiers straggled home, they brought the plague-carrying fleas with them in their infested clothes and luggage. The disease spread quickly, killing one out of five people. For the rest of the summer it raged over England, killing 3,000 people a week in London, and in the suburbs a total of 20,000 people.

Elizabeth was frustrated. She was angry with the French government, angry at the loss of Newhaven, and angry that Calais remained out of English hands. She became furious, though, when she heard people grumbling about female rulers being incompetent. One Englishman, complaining about Elizabeth and female rulers, prayed, "God help England and send it . . . a king."

Elizabeth had learned a hard lesson at Newhaven. But she was beginning to develop her own political strategy. By appointing Dudley as a rival councilor to Cecil, she now had the benefit of hearing more than one perspective. She would listen, then decide for herself. Elizabeth wanted it clear to everyone that her councilors were her servants, not her tutors. Dudley had helped lead her into the French conflict. Now, instead of listening solely to Dudley, she distinguished between her private life and her official responsibilities. Elizabeth would be hard pressed ever to commit English troops again, until there was a direct threat to English soil.

GOOD QUEEN BESS

Though Elizabeth had managed to avert a French invasion through Scotland, her cousin, Mary Queen of Scots, remained a dangerous threat. In 1560, her husband, King Francis II of France, died. Mary's formidable mother-in-law, Catherine de' Medici, turned her attention to her next son, the new king, and Mary eventually returned home to Scotland. Having failed to produce an heir, she was of no more use to France.

Although they had never met, Elizabeth and Mary shared the experience of being powerful female royalty. Elizabeth had developed into a self-reliant woman living in a man's world. While she loved fashionable clothes and trinkets, Elizabeth's eyes were quick and self-assured behind her jeweled fans. Whether boasting or swearing, she was swaggeringly confident. Mary, on the

Elizabeth's cousin and rival, Mary Queen of Scots.

other hand, was seeking a second marriage and hoping for a husband's strength and advice. She relied heavily on her advisors and had a trusting—some said gullible—nature that would lead her into trouble.

Soon, tensions between Elizabeth and Mary were running high. Mary's beauty and charm were renowned; Elizabeth was no longer the most sought-after female sovereign in Europe. Elizabeth's councilors renewed their pleas that she marry and produce heirs to thwart any attempt to usurp the throne.

Ever since Elizabeth's ascension in 1558, Mary had been claiming she was Elizabeth's rightful successor to the throne of England. While in France, urged on by her father-in-law, she had even worn the English coat of arms. Now she wanted Elizabeth to name her as heir. Elizabeth strung Mary along in order to maintain the upper hand. The idea of a Catholic foreigner with strong French ties eventually ruling England horrified her and her subjects and advisors. However, a few plotted to secure for Mary the English crown.

Mary began negotiations to marry Don Carlos, the heir to the Spanish throne. Although Don Carlos had suffered brain damage when he fell down a flight of stairs pursuing a maid, the marriage would weld Scotland to Catholic Spain. Elizabeth needed to make sure Mary didn't wed a strong Catholic prince.

Communicating with Mary by letters and through ambassadors, Elizabeth tried to delay the marriage. Marrying Don Carlos would be an overtly hostile act, she informed her cousin. Elizabeth and her councilors told Mary's secretary, William Maitland, they would not agree to any match with the Hapsburg family, either the Spanish or the Austrian branch.

Elizabeth proposed various acceptable husbands for Mary. She even suggested Robert Dudley. Many people thought this offer was insulting; Elizabeth seemed to be offering her a hand-me-down husband. As bait for the Dudley marriage, Elizabeth hinted she might consider Mary's claims as her heir. Mary tactfully said she couldn't deprive Elizabeth of Dudley's company. At the least, Elizabeth's move produced yet another delay in the ongoing game.

As Elizabeth would neither guarantee Mary's succession nor be content if she married anyone but an Englishman, Mary followed her heart. She had recently met the tall, handsome Henry Stuart, also known as Lord Darnley, who had traveled to Scotland hoping to woo her. Darnley fell ill during his visit, and Mary fell hopelessly in love with him.

Elizabeth was against the match for two reasons: Darnley was a Catholic, and his family was also descended from Margaret Tudor. His claim to the English throne was almost as strong as Mary's.

Although Elizabeth commanded Darnley back to England, he refused. Mary, too, refused to let Elizabeth stop the marriage but promised to wait three months before making a final decision. Just two months later, in July 1565, she and Darnley were married. Elizabeth was so upset she had Darnley's mother imprisoned in the Tower of London. Darnley was proclaimed king of Scotland. Mary and Darnley, both Catholic, now provided a double threat to England.

One year later, Mary gave birth to a son, James. Named as the baby's godmother, Elizabeth offered a promise to Mary. Provided Mary didn't press her claim to the English throne while Elizabeth was still alive, Elizabeth would ensure no laws were passed endangering Mary's claim. After years of worry and misunder-

Mary Queen of Scots *(right)* with her scheming husband, Lord Darnley. *(The National Trust)*

standings, it seemed at last Elizabeth and her cousin had made peace. Mary's claim to the English throne improved when it became clear she would not impose her Catholic faith on largely Protestant Scotland, suggesting she might rule England the same way one day. Also, as the mother of a son, she had an unquestionable heir—the throne would pass peacefully into his hands upon her death.

Elizabeth's councilors stepped up their pleas for her to marry and produce an heir, guaranteeing the succession through her line. They did not want succession to fall to the Stuarts. "There is a strong idea in the world that a woman cannot live unless she is married or at all events if she refrains from marriage she does so for some bad reason," Elizabeth complained to the Spanish ambassador.

Elizabeth told her councilors they failed to grasp the problem with naming her successor. People would look ahead to the next ruler instead of the current monarch. She artfully dodged her councilors' cries for marriage and continued to keep a tight rein on them, taking credit for successes and blaming them for failures.

Elizabeth had no shortage of difficult decisions at home and abroad. In 1564, the Netherlands had begun a revolt against the long-resented Catholic rule of King Philip II of Spain. The Netherlands consisted of seventeen socially, culturally, and linguistically divided provinces. The Catholic, southern areas spoke French and included the most urbanized portion of Europe and the great commercial city of Antwerp. The northern provinces, more agricultural and maritime, were increasingly Protestant.

From the beginning, the Dutch Protestants looked to Elizabeth for help. If she aided the rebels, she risked war with Spain. If she didn't, and the revolt was successful, the Dutch government might refuse to trade with an uncooperative England, which needed Dutch trade to prosper. The situation grew worse when Elizabeth ordered the seizure of a fleet of Spanish ships seeking shelter in English harbors from storms and Huguenot pirates. The fleet carried a huge sum of gold and silver coins, payment for the Spanish soldiers in the Netherlands. Always short of cash, Elizabeth confiscated the bounty. Though the Dutch offered Elizabeth regency of their new state, in the end the queen declined. Elizabeth did not want to get further financially involved in the quagmire of revolt in the Netherlands. England was, and always would be, her first priority.

Elizabeth worked relentlessly every day. She expected no less of those around her. Her councilors all were overworked and underpaid, but honored with high positions at court. Elizabeth watched her money closely, having inherited a nearly bankrupt kingdom. She ruled as she lived, with a strong sense of personal style. She was always the center of attention. Everyone spoke to her on bended knee. Courtiers were expected to forgo their own personal interests in exchange for the glory of serving her. Short of money, Elizabeth found other ways to reward hard work and loyalty, with gifts of land, expensive trinkets, and high appointments. She also offered exclusive licenses to sell goods and collect monies on imports and manufacturers. Those surrounding the queen pursued all of these plums endlessly.

Christopher Hatton was one man who learned the benefits of being in Elizabeth's favor. A handsome, talented jouster, Hatton first attracted Elizabeth's attention when he danced before her at a masque. By 1564, he had been made a royal bodyguard. A year later, the queen gave him a manor and other properties. Soon Hatton was knighted and became a member of the Privy Council. By 1587, he was Lord Chancellor. Hatton rose high because of Elizabeth's affections, and never forgot it. He showered her with loving letters. When they were apart for two days, he wrote, "I lack that I live by. . . . My wits are overwrought with thoughts. I find myself amazed. Bear with me most dear sweet lady. Passion overcometh me. I can write no more. Love me, for I love you. . . . Live for ever."

Sir Christopher Hatton in a miniature by Nicholas Hilliard. *(Victoria and Albert Museum, London)*

Courtiers attempted to outdo each other in praise of Elizabeth's beauty and splendor. They created songs, poems, and riddles complimenting her. One man even rebuilt his house in the shape of the letter "E" to prepare for the queen's visit. Sir Walter Raleigh, an adventurer, poet, and favorite of Elizabeth's, is said to have flattered the vain queen by spreading his costly new cloak over a mud puddle in order to protect her feet from the ground. She was amused by such flattery but also expected it. She gloried in the attention, setting the tone and mood for her court. Sometimes Elizabeth's life was a bit too public, though. "I do not live in a corner," she once said. "A thousand eyes see all I do."

Elizabeth rose around eight o'clock in the morning, much later than her 1,500 servants. She often worked late or amused herself into the night with cards or chess, and did not like mornings. When she was ready to dress, her ladies-in-waiting helped her into eight ornate layers of clothing. Beginning with a smock, they layered on top a bodice, petticoat, hoops, skirt, kirtle, gown, then finally laced or fastened on her sleeves. The bodice was mounted on a rigid wooden frame. It came to a point just below the hips, giving the illusion of a long torso and tiny waist.

Elizabeth's ladies curled and dressed her long red hair, filling it out with petards, or hairpieces. As she grew older and her hair thinned, Elizabeth wore extravagant red wigs in public. She carried a pomander, or container filled with herbs, to ward off foul smells. Elizabeth loved clothes and spent nearly £700 on them each year, outfitting herself with new French gowns, robes, cloaks, and skirts. Men and women at court spent so much on clothes they were said to wear their fortunes on their backs.

Elizabeth's gowns were encrusted with pearls, precious stones, and silver and gold thread. They were embroidered, trimmed with fur, or bejeweled in many different motifs. Some were decorated with pansies, her favorite flowers, or roses, suns, clouds, rainbows, feathers, pomegranates, or sea monsters. She loved silk stockings, wearing a new pair each week.

Elizabeth often used cosmetics to smooth and color

her skin. She relied on a combination of borax, alum, oil, and powdered eggshell to whiten her skin, as was the style. She wore red rouge and bright red lipstick. Many of the ingredients in cosmetics were dangerous. They

By the 1570s, when this portrait was painted, Elizabeth had cultivated the dramatic and commanding image for which she was renowned. *(National Portrait Gallery, London)*

contained lead and mercury, poisons that blackened teeth, coarsened skin, and destroyed the brain. The men at Elizabeth's court wore makeup as well. They even dyed their beards red, orange, purple, or gold-speckled to match their clothes.

After Elizabeth was dressed, unless it was raining, she took a fast walk alone through the formal gardens around her palaces. Elizabeth loved to walk in beautiful surroundings. All of her gardens had benches carved and painted with the royal arms. They also had wooden carvings of beasts on tall poles, providing a blaze of color and interest in winter. Elizabeth loved exercise. She often walked, danced, hunted with falcons, and rode horses.

Elizabeth had private meals in her own chamber. Few people ate breakfast. There were two main meals—dinner, around noon, and supper, in the evening. Elizabeth ate light meats, such as fish and fowl, and drank diluted sweet wine or beer with her meal. Everyone, even children, drank ale or beer with meals. The average person drank about a gallon of ale a day. Water was untreated—raw sewage and trash were dumped into rivers—so drinking beer was safer. Elizabeth ate with expensive knives, spoons, and jeweled toothpicks. Forks, recently invented in Italy, had not yet come to England. Drinking glasses, imported from other countries, were fashionable but costly. Elizabeth also enjoyed sweets, causing her to have frequent toothaches as she grew older. Having teeth pulled without anesthetics was a trial of the day.

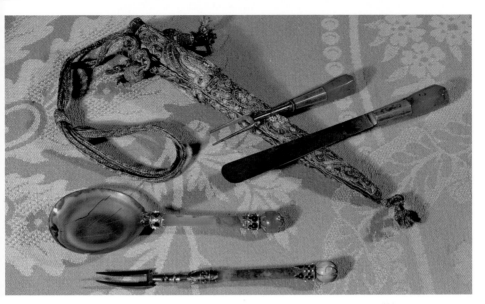

Travel cutlery and bag belonging to Queen Elizabeth. *(Courtesy of Art Resource.)*

The people of the court enjoyed tournaments, festivals, dances, and banquets. Elizabeth, always gorgeously dressed, made it a point to show herself among her people. She understood the importance of making a powerful public impression. The most lavish and glittering occasions at Elizabeth's court were the feasts and masques. These events often were given in outdoor banqueting houses, huge tents with canvas walls held up by ship masts. In June 1572, a French envoy visited and a huge banqueting house was constructed. Five hundred women decorated the tent with ivy, roses, and honeysuckle. The walls were painted to look like stone. The ceiling was painted and hung with artificial flowers and vegetables. The house was still in use twelve years later.

By sixteenth-century standards, Elizabeth was particular about her hygiene. She had a traveling bath, in which she bathed twice a year. She cleaned her teeth with cloths and gold toothpicks. She disliked strong smells, and special efforts were made to keep her houses clean. Even so, she needed to change her residence frequently so it could be cleaned.

In addition to the usual smells, London was sweltering and noisy in the summer. Food spoiled rapidly in the heat. The city was crowded and fleas spread the plague. Everyone knew London was unhealthy in the summer. Those who could get out did. Summers were an opportunity for Elizabeth to leave the city and visit her subjects. She needed to remain visible and she liked to observe the mood of the people and the state of her country. Thus, nearly every summer Elizabeth went on progress. Her servants loaded nearly six hundred wagons and 2,400 packhorses with the queen's luggage,

The impressively packed skyline of Elizabethan London, with the busy Thames, spanned by London Bridge, in the foreground. *(The British Library, London)*

England's Virgin Queen is carried in grand procession through the streets of London in this famous painting known as the *Blackfriar's Portrait*. *(Bridgeman Art Library, London)*

containing clothes, jewels, documents, dishes, utensils, and furniture. Everyone at court came along, from her councilors to her stablemen. It was an enormous under-taking.

A thirty-mile journey might take twelve hours. Horse-drawn carriages and covered wagons were introduced to England in the mid-sixteenth century, but they lacked springs and were an uncomfortable way to travel. Ladies wore travel masks to protect their complexions from the dust and dirt of the roads. The masks were kept in place by a button on the reverse side, which the women held between their teeth.

Elizabeth loved these trips. The train of wagons moved slowly through each small town. All along the route, Elizabeth allowed her subjects to approach her. She told them how much she loved them, and listened to the speeches and entertainment they had prepared. Elizabeth often rode open on horseback so her subjects could see her.

Elizabeth received gifts of cakes and flowers, and let people kiss her hand. Once, she stood in the rain to watch a child's play. Another time when fireworks planned for her entertainment burned down a man's house, she had it rebuilt. In one town, women prepared a banquet of 160 different foods. Elizabeth tasted them all, without having someone check them first for poisons, showing her trust in the people. Despite appearances, Elizabeth was always on guard. Her stops were planned ahead of time, but she constantly changed her travel plans, switching the route or bridge she was planning to take. Although these decisions frustrated Elizabeth's servants, it made ambushing the queen more difficult.

Some people gossiped that Elizabeth only went on progress to give birth to Dudley's children. Her life was too public for these rumors to have any truth. In general, Elizabeth was very popular with her subjects. However, the noblemen she stayed with on progresses weren't always happy. The cost of a visit from the queen could be staggering.

One reason Elizabeth went on progress was to save money. Her household alone cost £40,000 each year, downing 4 million eggs, 600,000 gallons of beer, and 20,000 sheep and lamb. Her financial obligations included supporting the court, paying for military expenses, paying the salaries of the government workers, constructing and maintaining buildings, and more, especially during emergencies.

Summer progresses forced some of Elizabeth's wealthier subjects to shoulder the costs of entertaining and feeding the court for a time. Elizabeth's wealthy hosts were required to feed three hundred guests for a week or more. Often when the court left, the area was stripped of game and livestock, and drained of ale and wine. People planned extravagant entertainment and banquets for Elizabeth's delight, and expanded their houses to accommodate her. Her servants camped in tents on the lawn.

Dudley and Cecil were among those who entertained Elizabeth in great style. They hosted the court on the magnificent estates Elizabeth had given them. Once, Dudley planned an immense fireworks display, trying to talk the pyrotechnician into launching dogs and cats whirling into the air. The man refused. Often people planned theatrical shows, such as mock sea battles, complete with armies of musicians and fantastic scenery, filled with symbolism honoring Elizabeth. They also presented her with rare and costly gifts.

As Elizabeth traveled through her realm, she could see that her people's lives were improving. They were wealthier and better educated than in medieval times. During Elizabeth's reign, the landowning class increased in prestige and wealth. There was a growing middle class of prosperous merchants, fueled by the sea exploration of both pirates and patriots.

The desire to find an English-controlled Northwest Passage to the spice and silk markets of Asia drove the exploration of North America. Although explorers like Martin Frobisher failed to find a practical passageway, they added to English knowledge of North America. In 1569, Dutch cartographer Gerhard Kremer, remembered as Mercator, published his revolutionary map representing the round world on a flat surface. Thrilling advances such as this prompted men like Sir Walter Raleigh to promote colonization of America. Raleigh established a colony at Roanoke, in present day North Carolina. He also named a region of the New World Virginia, in honor of Elizabeth, the Virgin Queen.

Voyages and exploration to Russia, the Middle East, Asia, and the Americas created new opportunities. People formed joint-stock companies, investing money and sharing profits with others. These companies established trade from Russia to the Indies.

English merchants traded in foreign luxuries such as French wines, Oriental spices, dried fruits from the Mediterranean, and gold and ivory from Africa. Costly imported spices obscured the taste of rotting meats. There was an increasing appetite for commodities obtained on one side of the Atlantic and sold on the other, such as African slaves. By the mid-sixteenth century, Europeans were enjoying potatoes, turkey, pineapple, avocados, chocolate, coffee, and tobacco from the New World.

Life in England was improving. Cottages that once had only primitive smoke holes in the ceilings now had chimneys. Straw pallets with rough sheets and no pillows had been replaced by beds, linens, blankets, and pillows. Pewter plates and utensils replaced wooden platters and spoons.

During Elizabeth's reign there were also less tangible improvements. There was a flowering of culture, supported and modeled by the queen herself. Art, theater, music, architecture, literature, and education flourished. By the end of her reign, Elizabeth had started 136 grammar schools. As the middle class became wealthier, they began to make more use of the printing presses that had been brought to England in the late sixteenth century. By the 1600s, three out of every ten men were literate, while in London the percentage was as high as seven out of ten.

Painting and art flowered as well. Limning, the art of miniature painting, became very popular. The English painter Nicholas Hilliard led the field, painting tiny, beautiful portraits using brushes made from squirrel hair. In Catholic countries, the church's demands for sumptuous displays of its glory led to a new trend in the arts called baroque, led by masters such as Michelangelo and Peter Paul Rubens.

It was also an age of aristocratic building. Architecture developed as great houses were restored or rebuilt. Elaborate gardens with vineyards and orchards surrounded these sprawling houses. Wealthy people filled their flower beds with rare and unusual plants.

A craze for instrumental chamber music spread over

England. Elizabeth instituted free concerts at the Royal Exchange in London, so that even the poor could share her love for music. Elizabeth enjoyed polyphonic church music, songs that had two or more independent voices, tunes, or melodies. Aristocrats followed Elizabeth's example and patronized musicians, commissioned new works, and collected instruments and printed music. When Puritans, who sought to remove ritual from worship, demanded this music be banned from churches, Elizabeth overrode them.

Puritan voices also sought to close theaters and prevent plays from being performed. But Elizabeth patronized the arts and protected artists when repressive forces threatened them. She formed her own theater company, the Queen's Men, and supported such artists as William

This nineteenth-century painting imagines Elizabeth watching Shakespeare's *The Merry Wives of Windsor* at the famed Globe Theatre. *(Courtesy of Art Resource.)*

Shakespeare and Christopher Marlowe, offering friendship and financial support. Greek and Roman histories, Italian romances, English kings and warriors, street ballads, and folk traditions inspired the plays of the day, which appealed to the masses of people who still were not readers.

An increasing interest in antiquarianism, or collecting artifacts of British history, swept through England. This enthusiasm for history fueled studies in science, economics, philosophy, geography, and mathematics. Great men such as John Dee gave popular public lectures sharing their findings. Dee even opened up his extensive library of navigational and astronomical instruments for study. Others, including Sir Thomas Bodley, founded Oxford University's Bodleian Library, and began to restore and expand its collections, creating England's first national library.

The centerpiece of England's glory was its glittering queen. She was known affectionately by many nicknames: people called her Good Queen Bess, for her fairness and kindness to her subjects. She also was known as Fair Eliza, for her beauty. Others called her Regina Gloriana, after a glorious fairy queen created by the poet Edmund Spenser.

Henry VIII's daughter had proven herself worthy of her father's mantle. Under her stewardship, England had achieved a time of unprecedented wealth and accomplishment. The one thing the queen could not do was quash concerns about the future of England once her reign was over.

REBELLION

Within a few months of Mary Queen of Scot's wedding, it was clear that she had made a mistake. Darnley, bitter about not being crowned king, drank too much, got in fights, and had affairs. Mary withdrew into her work, and Darnley spent most of his time hunting.

Mary had other problems. A faction of Protestant aristocrats led by her half brother, the Earl of Moray, were mounting a plot against the throne. When Elizabeth refused Moray aid, the rebellion was quickly put down by Mary's army.

During this time, Mary frequently sought the advice and counsel of her secretary, David Rizzio. An Italian singer, Rizzio was generally disliked. His increasing power at court gave rise to rumors that he and Mary were lovers. Mary did not realize that her affection for Rizzio was costing her public support—even her Catholic husband, angry at what he saw as Mary's betrayal, promised to aid her Protestant enemies. Darnley was particularly enraged by the rumors that Mary's recently announced pregnancy might have been fathered by Rizzio.

The hotheaded Darnley was lured into a plot to murder Rizzio.

David Rizzio, advisor to Mary Queen of Scots.

Most likely directed by the Earl of Moray from behind the scenes, Darnley and some of his followers broke into a room where the Italian was eating dinner with Mary and stabbed him to death. Mary was horrified but realized what her husband had not—that the men behind the plot planned to get Darnley out of the way next. Mary saved Darnley's life, but soon she learned the extent to which he had plotted against her.

When Elizabeth heard about Rizzio's murder, and how Mary was facing plots from all sides, she was sympathetic to her cousin's plight. Elizabeth knew that Mary's mental and physical health were declining.

Darnley, who was now living with his father in Glasgow, fell ill with syphilis. In January 1567, Mary brought him back to Edinburgh to convalesce. On February 10, an explosion rocked Kirk o' Field, the house where Darnley was sleeping. He and his servant were found dead under a tree. They had both been strangled and had no marks from the blast—it was clear the explosion was meant to cover up their murders.

Mary had attended a wedding earlier that evening, left her husband at Kirk o' Field, and went to sleep at the nearby palace of Holyrood. James Hepburn, the Earl of Bothwell, seemed the most likely candidate to have carried out the murders, but he was acquitted in a sham trial. Though Mary swore she had nothing to do with Darnley's death, most people were unconvinced. Then, just three months after Darnley was killed, Mary and Bothwell were married.

Rumors flew around Europe. How much had Mary known about the plot to kill her husband? Certainly, she had tolerated the murder, if she hadn't been actively involved. The pope denounced her. Her own countrymen imprisoned her at the island castle of Lochleven. Bothwell escaped to Denmark, where he was imprisoned and later died. Mary was forced to abdicate her throne to her infant son, James.

In May 1568, Mary escaped prison. Cutting her hair and assuming a disguise, she made her way into England. She hoped her cousin Elizabeth would help her. But having another queen on English soil, and one who claimed the English throne, created a situation rife with danger for Elizabeth.

She and her advisors weighed their options. They could return Mary to her captors, but Elizabeth worried this would seriously undermine royalty everywhere, weakening her own power. Another option was to restore Mary to her throne, possibly sparking a war in Protestant Scotland. The war might involve France, too, because of Mary's French ties. A third possibility was to imprison Mary in England, angering Catholics everywhere. A fourth choice was to release Mary to the French, but she might gain enough support there to invade Scotland. Yet another solution was to let Mary go free in England, where she might raise support for her own claim to the English throne. Each one of these options had drawbacks. In the meantime, Mary was confined to a castle in the distant north of England. Suspicion about her involvement in Darnley's murder meant Elizabeth could not receive her at court.

Elizabeth was well aware that several Catholic rulers were greedily eyeing England, and that Mary was the keystone of their plots. France, though still shaken by civil war, might use Mary as an excuse to seize both Scotland and England. Catholic Spain's leading soldier, the Duke of Alva, had recently brought 10,000 soldiers to occupy the Netherlands where nearly 25,000 soldiers from Germany, Italy, and Belgium added to his forces. A potential invading army was camped on England's doorstep.

Elizabeth's advisors wanted her to marry immediately and produce an heir, or to recognize Mary as her successor. They thought Mary would be a tolerant ruler, and were glad that she had an heir in her son James. A group of noblemen, including Robert Dudley, concerned about the succession and indignant at Elizabeth's autonomy as queen, orchestrated a plan that hinged on Elizabeth's councilor, the Duke of Norfolk, and Mary.

Norfolk was England's only duke. Closely related to three queens, including Elizabeth, Norfolk lived like a king. Thousands of tenants inhabited his sprawling lands. At the snap of his fingers, he could raise a large army. Wealthy and ambitious, Norfolk believed it was his destiny to become Mary's husband and the future king of England.

Thomas Howard, the fourth Duke of Norfolk.

Dudley and his allies planned to restore Mary to the Scottish throne and to ensure her succession in England. In return, Mary would wed Norfolk, maintain

Mary Queen of Scots with her young son, James.

Protestantism in Scotland, and become England's ally. She agreed to the plot.

Elizabeth was most likely aware of the plot from the beginning, thanks to her vast network of spies. In her typical fashion, she waited to see what would develop before taking action. Having Mary restored to the Scottish throne was not unappealing—it would get her troublesome cousin out of England. But she worried about Norfolk's ambition. Once he took Scotland, what would keep him from moving on England?

In the end, the plot was aborted when the conspirators lost their nerve. Dudley confessed the plan to Elizabeth, guessing correctly that her love for him would guarantee his forgiveness. Norfolk was arrested in October of 1569 and imprisoned in the Tower of London.

For months, unrest had been brewing in predominantly Catholic northern England. Norfolk's imprisonment sparked a revolt, as he had many powerful allies in the region. Since Mary was still on English soil, these Catholic rebels hoped to liberate her and overthrow Elizabeth and her Protestant government. They were encouraged by the promise of Spanish support.

As the Catholic army marched south, Elizabeth prepared Windsor Castle for a siege and had Mary moved farther away. But by December 20, the uprising had collapsed. Chased by a strong royal army, the leaders escaped into Scotland. Nearly 750 rebels were hanged.

Outraged by the failure of the Northern Rising, on February 25, 1570, Pope Pius V issued a statement denouncing "Elizabeth, the pretended Queen of England, the servant of wickedness." The pope absolved Elizabeth's subjects of their allegiance to her. Now English Catholics no longer could be good Catholics and good Englishmen at the same time. She was officially excommunicated and labeled a heretic queen who should be dethroned. It was an open invitation for the Catholics of Europe to join together to overthrow Elizabeth and return England to Catholicism. Mary Queen of Scots confided to the Spanish ambassador's servant that with Philip II's aid, she would be queen of England within three months.

Fortunately, most English Catholics were comfortable having Elizabeth as their sovereign and the pope as their spiritual leader. Elizabeth did not want to persecute her subjects by tightening laws against Catholics. But the pope had forced her hand; she had to do something.

Her Parliament met in April and passed two bills. One made it traitorous to introduce papal bulls, or formal documents from the pope, into the realm, and to call Elizabeth a tyrant or heretic. The second bill stated that anyone who tried to usurp the throne of England would forfeit any right to succession.

In January 1571, another conspiracy against Elizabeth began to take shape. The Ridolfi plot was the inspiration of the banker Roberto Ridolfi, an Italian based in London. Ridolfi planned to have Spanish troops in the Netherlands invade England. At the same time, English Catholics would rise up and the rebels would free Mary, seize Elizabeth, and wed Mary to Norfolk. When news of the plot reached the English government, Norfolk, Ridolfi, and Mary's diplomatic agent, John Leslie, were quickly implicated. English subjects and councilors began to call for Mary's execution.

Mary claimed she was innocent of any intrigue. But through her extensive spy network, Elizabeth kept track of Mary's actions. She considered Mary to be the cause of many of her problems.

The king of Spain's eagerness to support English rebels concerned Elizabeth. Philip's hostility towards her was increasing as they also battled over ownership of territories in the Americas. In 1493, the pope had divided these lands between Spain and Portugal. Now those two countries forbid foreign merchants to visit the territories or trade with them. Silver and gold flowed out of Spanish America in treasure-laden ships. For years,

England resented not being able to share in these riches. Elizabeth began to sponsor privateers, official pirates, to attack any ship from Spanish America.

In February 1571, the Earl of Morton, a lord of Scotland's child-king James, arrived in England to discuss Mary's fate. When Morton said he couldn't accept any proposal weakening James's power, Elizabeth pretended to be furious. After four years of disputes, the project to restore Mary to the throne of Scotland ground to a halt. It was clear that predominately Protestant Scotland did not want Mary back. Elizabeth did not want her return to power either, fearing she would press her claim to the English throne. The wisest choice was to delay, to do nothing. Even though many councilors and subjects pushed for Mary's execution, Elizabeth stalled. She worried that proceeding against a fellow queen could undermine her own power.

After an agonizing and scandalous inquiry into Darnley's death, the revelation of the so-called Casket Letters—purportedly from Mary to Bothwell—forced an English tribunal to declare it could not find her innocent of a conspiracy to kill her husband. Mary claimed the letters were forgeries, but was placed under house arrest. Elizabeth knew that to hold Mary captive was to risk the wrath of both France and Spain. But when a French ambassador spoke up in Mary's favor, Elizabeth said Mary was "the worst woman in the world, whose head should have been cut off years ago," adding that Mary "would never be free as long as she lived."

Elizabeth's relations with both France and Spain were souring. In 1572, Catherine de' Medici ordered the St. Bartholomew's Day Massacre. Thousands of French Huguenots were murdered in a bloody purge. Elizabeth and Protestants everywhere were shocked and horrified. Philip II spoke for Catholic Europe when he called it "one of the greatest joys of my life."

At forty-five years old, Elizabeth was no longer a young woman. The chances of her bearing an heir were slim. Technically, though, she was an eligible bride. Hoping to improve relations with France and Spain, Elizabeth embarked on yet another personal and political flirtation and came closer to marriage than ever before.

Francis of Valois, the Duke of Alençon, was Catherine de' Medici's youngest son and in line for the throne of France. But the duke was hungry for power and had plotted with the Huguenots against his mother and brother. Alençon had much to gain from a marriage to Elizabeth. While the French government was preoccupied by religious strife, Alençon had made an agreement with the Dutch. In return for his military assistance, he was named protector of the Netherlands. The duke hoped a marriage with Elizabeth would provide him with the funding and influence he needed.

Elizabeth and Alençon began to exchange love letters and tokens. The queen spoke eagerly about meeting the duke in person. No one was more surprised by the seeming honesty of Elizabeth's infatuation than Robert

Dudley. Jealous, Dudley spread the rumor that the French were using love potions on Elizabeth.

Everyone wondered if Elizabeth would want to marry the duke once she saw him. Alençon was short and extremely ugly, his face badly scarred from smallpox. Only twenty-five, he was nearly half Elizabeth's age. Despite his support for the Huguenots,

Francis of Valois, Duke of Alençon.

the French duke was also Catholic. Elizabeth was prepared to overlook both the duke's religion and his demand to be crowned king once they were married.

For over twenty years, Elizabeth's advisors had begged her to marry. Yet the closer this marriage loomed, the more dangerous it seemed. Angry pamphlets denouncing closer ties with France were left for Elizabeth to find. Preachers thundered about the evils of marrying a foreigner and a Catholic. One day, as Elizabeth traveled in her barge, a gunshot hit one of the royal bargeman sitting just a few feet away.

The greatest act of treachery came from one of Elizabeth's most trusted and beloved courtiers. In 1578, Robert Dudley secretly married Lettice Knollys. For years, Dudley had hoped to wed Elizabeth and become king. Now he wanted to marry and have an heir to carry on his family name. Elizabeth discovered Dudley's marriage just weeks before Alençon arrived. Deeply wounded, Elizabeth felt Dudley had committed a personal rebellion. She saw her flirtation with the duke as an opportunity to punish Dudley.

Alençon "secretly" arrived in England on August 17, 1579, although everyone at court knew he was there. Elizabeth nicknamed him her "Frog." She loved the intrigue and the secrecy of his visit and especially the attentions of the young duke.

All of Europe followed the queen's budding romance. No one knew whether Elizabeth was serious or leading everyone along in a merry dance. "I have always looked upon the idea of a marriage between the queen and Alençon as a mere invention," Philip II wrote. "I nevertheless believe they will continue to discuss it, and even may become reconciled for the purpose, but I believe that she herself is the person who will refuse."

Elizabeth strung Alençon along for three years. Finally, during Alençon's return visit to England, he got his answer. On November 22, 1581, Elizabeth told the French ambassador, "You may write this to the king: that the Duke of Alençon shall be my husband!" She gave Alençon one of her rings and kissed him on the mouth.

He handed one of his rings to Elizabeth. Elizabeth then summoned all of her courtiers and repeated her vow before them. Dudley was upset and Christopher Hatton wept. The ladies of the court were hysterical. All of England thought this marriage would ruin their realm. When Elizabeth saw how her subjects would react to the duke as a ruler, she withdrew her promise.

Alençon cursed women and islanders but stayed in England. He began to demand large payments from Elizabeth to support the Protestant Netherlands. The duke felt Elizabeth owed him some compensation for all her empty promises. Alençon began to bully Elizabeth. "If I cannot get you for my wife by fair means and affection I must do so by force, for I will not leave this country without you," he threatened. During the day he pretended to swoon with love for her, while at night he visited London brothels.

Any remaining interest Elizabeth had in the marriage was gone. She offered a loan for the war in the Netherlands, with the qualifier that France would have to come to England's aid if Spain invaded England. In January 1582, Elizabeth gave Alençon an advance on the loan, hoping it would encourage him to leave for the Netherlands.

One month later, Alençon set off. Dudley accompanied him, at the head of an English army. As they sailed out of sight, Elizabeth felt torn. Alençon had been her last hope for marriage, and now he was leaving, never to return.

In the Netherlands, Alençon was made the Duke of

Brabant, the ruler of the Low Countries. But he failed to take immediate action against the Spanish forces. The duke claimed to be waiting for French reinforcements. Once the reinforcements arrived, he turned traitor and attempted to seize Antwerp, but was defeated. By June of 1583, he was home in France. One year later he died of a fever, leaving the Dutch without a ruler and France without a Catholic heir.

Alençon had proven to be treacherous and incompetent. While Elizabeth had avoided marrying him, her flirtation with the idea had earned the hostility of Spain and lost the support of France. Her only allies were the weak rebel provinces in the Netherlands, and this was more of an obligation than a support. In the 1585 Treaty of Nonsuch, Elizabeth made a formal alliance with the Netherlands against Spain. She fully committed England to the Dutch cause, supplying more soldiers and horses. With the recent deaths of Alençon and William of Orange, the Protestant rebels needed a new leader. Elizabeth sent Robert Dudley to fill the void.

Fifty years old, past her marriageable and childbearing years, Elizabeth began to cultivate another image for herself. She understood the importance of appearances and symbolism. Elizabeth became known as the Virgin Queen, married solely to England. Symbols from medieval literature, including the rose, the pearl, and the moon, were used to describe her purity and beauty. She was compared to mythological women such as Astrea, who fled the Earth because of mankind's wickedness.

Much also was made of Elizabeth's alleged ancestor, the legendary King Arthur. Imagery and myths spun around her, creating an aura of divinity.

The Virgin Queen's Catholic enemies saw her as an evil, controlling heretic and championed another woman—Mary Queen of Scots.

One of Elizabeth's advisors, Francis Walsingham, a strict Puritan, foresaw Catholic powers launching an assault on England and believed Mary was Elizabeth's gravest danger. He used his intelligence and knowledge of foreign courts and languages to seek out plots, at home and abroad. Walsingham was determined to prove Mary was plotting against the queen.

Walsingham's spy network caught one of Mary's spies, Gilbert Gifford. Walsingham used him to discover the contents of Mary's secret letters. Gifford took the letters from Mary's friends to the brewer who supplied her beer. The letters were wrapped in a watertight case and slipped in the beer barrel before it was

The queen's stern-faced advisor, Sir Francis Walsingham.

delivered to Mary's castle. Mary's written responses took the same journey, right into Walsingham's hands. Experts decoded the letters, resealed the wax seals, and sent them on their way. Walsingham sat back and waited.

Mary soon fell into the trap. A group of men conspiring against Elizabeth wrote to Mary, who approved their plot in writing and gave them advice. Fourteen conspirators were eventually caught and executed. Walsingham also read correspondences between Mary and Philip II in which Philip told Mary he was preparing to send his Armada to set her free.

Finally, Walsingham had enough evidence of Mary's plotting to convince Elizabeth that it was time to move. Faced with the proof, Elizabeth had no choice. Mary was tried for treason. The Queen of Scots was convicted and sentenced to death.

For months, Elizabeth refused to sign Mary's death warrant. She didn't want to be the one responsible for authorizing the death of a fellow female monarch. Further, Elizabeth feared retribution from France, Spain, and Scotland if she had Mary executed. Then another plot on Elizabeth's life was uncovered. The French ambassador and others had made plans to kill her either by poison or gunpowder, in order to place Mary on the throne. Finally, Elizabeth realized that if she saved Mary, she would be destroying herself. Mary is "the serpent that poisons me," Elizabeth wrote. On February 1, 1587, she signed the death warrant. Mary was beheaded seven days later, after spending nineteen years under house arrest.

When Mary's execution was announced to Elizabeth, she wept with rage and sorrow for herself and her cousin. She feared retribution from God and from other countries. She tried to blame the decision on her councilors, attempting to save her international reputation and assuage her own guilt. But no one believed her. "It is very fine for the Queen of England now to give out that it was done without her wish, the contrary so clearly being the case," said Philip II.

Elizabeth wrote to James VI of Scotland, Mary's son, calling Mary's death a "miserable accident." James, who had grown up without his mother, issued only a token protest. While people in Scotland were outraged at Mary's execution, James was anxious to avoid war and couldn't

Mary Queen of Scots was tried and beheaded at Fotheringhay Castle in central England, where her body lay for months before being buried at Peterborough Cathedral. During his reign, Mary's son, James, had her body exhumed and reburied at Westminster Abbey. (Scottish National Portrait Gallery, Edinburgh)

afford to alienate Elizabeth. He was next in line for her throne. The Earl of Moray sold Elizabeth some of Mary's jewelry. Elizabeth bought strands of valuable black and white pearls as large as grapes.

As Elizabeth had feared, Mary's execution infuriated Catholic Europe. An English ambassador reported, "I never saw a thing more hated by little, great, old, young, and of all religions than the Queen of Scots' death." Henry III of France condemned Mary's execution. The nation dressed in black mourning clothes and cried for Mary to be named a saint. But this was just talk—France had too many internal problems to seriously consider avenging Mary's death.

More ominously, the pope called for a crusade against Elizabeth and urged Spain to invade England. Philip II needed little encouragement. He had watched the events unfolding in the Netherlands with a growing distrust of Elizabeth. Philip's hopes for overthrowing Elizabeth by subterfuge died when Mary was executed. Now, he produced a will he claimed was made by Elizabeth's sister Mary in which she had given Scotland to him. Based on his claim, he could also claim the throne of England.

After years of increasing tensions between the two countries, Philip II pledged a holy crusade against the heretic Queen Elizabeth. He would use his mighty Armada to crush the tiny island nation.

7

WAR WITH SPAIN

As Elizabeth's former brother-in-law, Philip II, planned to invade England, led by the most powerful navy ever to sail the high seas, English spies in Spain kept her informed of Philip's plans.

The austere, monk-like Philip II never approved of Elizabeth as a potential wife or as a queen. She was Protestant; he saw himself as the savior of Catholicism. They clashed over Mary Queen of Scots, the Netherlands, and the Americas. For years Elizabeth's privateers had harassed Philip's ships, stealing their cargoes. In 1577, Elizabeth approved Francis Drake's attempt to circumnavigate the globe. Drake returned three years later, his ships laden with Spanish treasure from the unguarded towns he attacked along the South American coast. He was praised as a national hero when he un-

Sir Francis Drake.

loaded the two hundred tons of gold and silver stolen from Spain. Elizabeth knighted him in 1581.

Drake's exploits had lifted the country's morale and boosted the nation's confidence in the skill and daring of English seamen. England's burgeoning seafaring tradition would help sustain the country in the coming struggle with Spain.

Philip wanted revenge for all of these provocations, and he was in a position to exact it. Spain was the heart of a world empire that included parts of Italy, the Neth-

Spain's Armada was feared throughout the world for its heavily armed and powerful warships. *(National Maritime Museum, Greenwich, UK)*

erlands, the West Indies, and large portions of North and South America, Africa, and Asia. In 1581, Philip had annexed Portugal, combining two maritime powers. He was wealthier than all of the European sovereigns combined. The Spanish Armada, his unparalleled fleet of warships, carried 30,000 men ready to set sail, unload, and march to London.

Philip's Armada spent the winter of 1587 gathering supplies at the Spanish port of Cadiz. An invasion was planned for August, when food would be abundant in the English countryside. Elizabeth's councilors begged her to act, but she waited, still hoping to avoid war. Finally, she sent Francis Drake to sea to try to stop the mighty Armada.

In April, Drake set sail with two dozen ships. Ten days

later, Elizabeth had second thoughts and tried to call him back. It was too late. On April 19, Drake rode straight into Cadiz with cannons booming. He burned or sank nearly thirty-seven warships and smaller boats. Drake's men also destroyed shiploads of hoops and seasoned wood needed to make barrels to carry the Armada's food and water. Then Drake, whom the Spanish called El Draque, "the Dragon," dashed for the Azores, a group of Portuguese Islands. He led the Spanish on a wild-goose chase, eventually capturing a Spanish ship containing £100,000 worth of cargo. Drake modestly said he had done no more than "singe the King of Spain's beard." But he had bought England nearly a year's worth of time. Spain's preparations were so disrupted that their invasion was postponed until 1588.

Both England and Spain hurried to build up their navies. While Drake had destroyed many Spanish ships, the greater loss was actually the lumber for the barrels. The ships could be replaced. The seasoned lumber could not. The Spaniards had to use green wood for new barrels, which leaked, and caused the food and water to spoil quickly. The new ships were gigantic but awkward, with hastily built, untested cannons. They carried too few guns, and didn't have enough gunners to man them.

Still, Philip was so proud of his gargantuan fleet he published lists describing his ships, their guns, and the crew. Eager to paint the Spaniards as monsters, printers in Amsterdam embellished the list by including the Spanish instruments of torture and adding wild stories about how the Spaniards would torture and kill all English adults and put their children in the care of an army of Spanish nurses carried in the holds of their ships.

Though England was an island nation, the number of ships in Elizabeth's fleet was relatively small. Henry VIII, who loved the sea and ships, had begun building the English navy. But Edward and Mary had let the fleet diminish. Elizabeth had thirty-four new ships built to reinforce her fleet. These nimble vessels were among the fastest in the world. Holding more cannons than troops, the ships were speedy, maneuverable platforms for heavy guns and had a more modern design than the Spanish ships. They also had long-range guns on the sides, along with better-trained captains and seamen.

The ships in the English Royal Navy were painted bright colors and had names such as *Triumph* and *Revenge,* while the Spanish ships were named for religious saints such as *San Francesco* and *San Luis.* Holy images and crusading crosses were painted on every flag in the Spanish Armada. The flagship's banner had a crucified Christ on one side and the Virgin Mary on the other. Nearly two hundred monks sailed with the Armada to perform daily mass and prayer. At sunrise and sunset, the Spanish sailors all sang religious hymns, reminding them that this was a holy war, and God was on their side.

Elizabeth also needed to create an army. A standing army was costly to maintain. The 50,000 soldiers mustered to fight off Spanish invaders were poorly trained. They faced a disciplined Spanish army of at least 40,000 men. In London, an army of 29,000 men served as Elizabeth's personal defense force.

Elizabeth ordered defensive measures, including platform barriers built along bends in the Thames River as it wound through London. Soldiers could deliver a barrage of gunfire on passing enemy ships. One thousand tall iron poles were erected along hilltops from the southern coast of England to London and the Scottish border. On the top of the poles were baskets containing tar-soaked flammable wood. As soon as someone saw an enemy ship approaching, the beacons could be lit, one after another, sending an alarm across the country. Cattle grazing near the sea were driven inland to prevent them from becoming food for Spanish sailors. Heavy chains, held in place by small boats anchored in the river, were locked together and stretched across the Thames.

The Spanish Armada sailed from Lisbon in early May of 1588. Church bells rang out to celebrate their holy crusade. Almost immediately, the Spanish fleet met a series of disasters. First, winds blew many of the ships off course. The Armada had to travel slowly to stay near its heavily laden supply ships. The Spanish sailors began to fall sick from drinking foul water and eating spoiled food. They opened barrel after barrel and found each one to be stinking and crawling with worms. Only the rice was unspoiled. The green barrel staves were destroying their food supplies.

June, usually the best sailing month, was even worse than May. As the Spanish admiral, the Duke of Medina

Sidonia, was about to call a halt to the expedition, a storm arose. The ships were scattered and some were seriously damaged. The fleet limped into the harbor of Corunna in northwestern Spain. King Philip ordered them to proceed. God would be on their side, he said. On July 12, with boats repaired and sailors fed, they weighed anchor and set off for the coast of England again.

A week later, on the afternoon of July 19, an English captain saw the first Spanish sail. By evening the beacon fires were burning. Within hours the chain of warning lights had spread far across the north and west. By morning it had reached the border of Scotland. The time for the great battle was drawing nearer. Three days later, most of the English ships had been launched from Plymouth harbor.

The English fleet trailed behind the Armada, which stretched out in a crescent shape two miles wide. For now, Drake and the English commander, Charles Howard, were content with pestering the Spanish fleet. The Span-

The Spanish Armada proceeds up the coast of the British Isles in its protective crescent. *(Library of Congress)*

ish fleet had 130 vessels, compared to England's 105. The hulking Spanish warships were designed to make it easy to board enemy ships. If they got close enough, hundreds of armed fighters could pour down platforms onto the smaller English ships. The Armada carried more than 30,000 troops, twice the number aboard the English ships. But the Armada was weighed down by dozens of supply ships carrying troops, horses, and weapons, which gave the English a critical advantage in speed. The English swept around either flank of the Armada, firing upon them from afar for hours.

One of the Spanish warships caught fire and its gunpowder exploded, killing two hundred men. A second Spanish ship, the *Rosario*, was damaged when it collided with another. Drake overtook it during the night and forced its surrender. He welcomed the Spanish commander on board his own ship, the *Revenge*, while his men seized the thousands of gold ducats the Spanish ship had been carrying.

Slowly, under constant pressure from the English, the Spanish Armada sailed up the coast of England and anchored off of Calais on July 27. They had orders from King Philip to wait for the Duke of Parma, who was bringing an invasion force from the Netherlands. Parma's barges were held up by attacks from the Dutch Protestants and did not arrive for days. The Spanish fleet waited impatiently for their rendezvous.

Philip II had been careful to ensure that France would not come to England's aid during the war. He sent money to the Guise family, who saw themselves as the defenders of the Catholic faith in France, to be used to fund yet another religious conflict in the war-torn nation. France was reduced to chaos and neared total disintegration. England would have to stand alone against Spain.

While the Armada waited, poised to invade, the English attacked. On the night of July 28, 1588, English sailors loaded eight small ships with tar, twigs, and gunpowder. They lit these flammable materials, then launched the "hellburners." When the ships exploded, the Spanish had to cut their anchors loose to escape. Unable to moor again, the ships scattered. At dawn, as Medina Sidonia attempted to round up his Armada, the English attacked.

Blasting away, Drake's *Revenge* closed in on Medina Sidonia's ship, the *San Martin*. As the battle around them blazed, the *San Martin* took two hundred shots to the starboard side alone. While the Spanish admiral's ship remained afloat, the rest of the Armada took a beating. At least one thousand Spanish sailors died before the English ran out of ammunition nine hours later. At times, the ships were so close the sailors could shout back and forth, hurling insults at each other. At such close range, despite the wind and a thick fog, the English cannons pierced huge holes in the hulls of the Spanish ships. Spanish divers patched the holes as fast as they could, but it wasn't enough. After the battle, winds blew the Armada into the North Sea, off the course of their rendezvous with Parma.

On August 8, Elizabeth sailed to Tilbury, the head-

On the night of July 28, 1588, the Spanish and English navies engaged in fiery combat off the port of Calais in the English Channel.

quarters of the English land forces, on her royal barge. Dudley was the commander of Tilbury Camp, near London. As trumpets and drum rolls announced Elizabeth's arrival in the camp, a happy shout went up from the men. Elizabeth rode in among them on a huge white warhorse. Armed like a great warrior queen, she wore white velvet. Plumes of feathers, like the ones on the helmets of her mounted soldiers, adorned her hair. Every man Elizabeth passed fell to his knees in reverence.

In the weeks following the sighting of the first Spanish ship, little word had come about the fate of either country's fleet. Elizabeth's arrival encouraged the men. They knew they were in peril if England's navy fell. Everyone feared Spain would land in England any day and begin a bloody invasion, surging toward London.

Elizabeth rode through the camp again the following day. She made one of the greatest speeches of her life, appealing to her subjects' patriotism and to their affection for her: "I have placed my chiefest strength and safeguard in the loyal hearts and good will of my subjects; and therefore I am come amongst you as you see, at this time, not for my recreation and disport, but being resolved, in the midst and heat of the battle, to live or die amongst you all, and to lay down for my God and for my kingdom and for my people, my honor and my blood,

Queen Elizabeth rides to Tilbury to encourage the British troops and pledge her confidence in an English victory over Spain. (*St. Faith's Church, Norfolk*)

even in the dust," she told them. Cheers from her soldiers interrupted Elizabeth's words. "I know I have the body of a weak and feeble woman," she went on, "but I have the heart and stomach of a king, and of a king of England too, and think foul scorn that Parma or Spain, or any prince of Europe should dare to invade the borders of my realm; to which, rather than any dishonor shall grow by me, I myself will take up arms, I myself will be your general, judge, and rewarder of every one of your virtues in the field."

Elizabeth's speech ended to her army's thunderous applause. The bravery and confidence of this thin, aging woman appealed to her subjects once again. She set her subjects' hearts burning with the desire for glory.

Dudley believed Elizabeth's speech had "so inflamed the hearts of her good subjects, as I think the weakest among them is able to match the proudest Spaniard that dares land in England."

Although Elizabeth did not yet know it, the war was already over. After suffering terrible losses, Medina Sidonia had little choice but to abandon the holy crusade against England. Spain had long been Europe's greatest sea power, but a new era of English naval power was dawning. The battle near Calais was the end of Spain's rule of the seas.

Still, sailors worried the Armada had holed up in Denmark to refit its boats. English seamen continued to stand guard, despite illness from the rough seas and drinking sour beer. Fresh water ran out and they were forced to drink their own urine. Hundreds began to die from typhus, an infectious disease carried by lice and fleas. Still, they waited for Spain to reappear.

All of Europe waited, uncertain. Bells rang in Catholic cities as false rumors spread of Drake's capture, massive English losses, and Spanish victory. In Spain, crowds rejoiced around bonfires, celebrating the defeat of the wicked heretic queen.

As the once-glorious Armada limped home, Spain's bad luck continued. Storms ravaged the battle-torn Armada as it sailed around Scotland and Ireland. To lighten their loads, and to preserve more food and water, captains threw overboard the horses and mules planned for use in the invasion. By this time, much of their food was rancid. Many of the ships were riding low in the water or sinking. New storms drove ships aground, where the sailors were captured and executed. Nearly half of the Spanish Armada's men had been drowned, starved, died of disease, or killed.

Not for weeks was it known for sure in England that Spain had been defeated. Gradually, the truth became clear as dead sailors, horses, mules, and wrecked Spanish galleons continued to wash ashore. Three months after the battle at Calais, the evidence of Spain's defeat was indisputable. As Geoffrey Fenton walked on the coast of Ireland, he counted more than eleven hundred Spanish corpses washed up on the beach in less than five miles.

When Elizabeth heard the news of the Spanish retreat, rumor has it she rode her horse up the stairs of a hunting lodge in joy. England was saved. Protestants everywhere celebrated Spain's defeat. "She came, she saw, she fled," mocked one pamphlet. There was a growing national confidence in England. The Protestants became convinced that God had intervened in their favor.

All of Europe had considered Spain undefeatable. Much credit for the victory was given to Elizabeth. Her reputation soared. Even her enemies praised her. Pope Sixtus V said, "She certainly is a great queen, and were she only a Catholic, she would be our dearly beloved. Just look how well she governs! She is only a woman, only mistress of half an island, and yet she makes herself feared by Spain, by France, by all!" The pope even joked he would like to marry Elizabeth, stating that their children would rule the world.

As national celebrations continued in England, Philip II was decimated by his defeat. He retreated to the Escorial, his cavernous palace near Madrid. At the core of the Escorial was a monastery where Philip consoled himself with prayer. People in Spain put on mourning clothes and walked the streets with their heads bent in shame.

In England, the legend of the Virgin Queen spread. Elizabeth's subjects basked in the glow of their victory. John Sly, a schoolboy, expressed the mood of the English people when he scribbled Elizabeth's name in his Latin textbook and wrote:

"The rose is red, the leaves are green,
God Save Elizabeth, our noble Queen!"

8

TREASURES AND TREASON

Elizabeth had just a few short weeks to gloat over her glorious victory against Spain and to enjoy her improved reputation throughout Europe. In the autumn of 1588, she experienced a terrible personal loss that made the victory seem bittersweet. Robert Dudley, the Earl of Leicester, passed away.

Dudley was fifty-five when he died, old for the times. The last few months had exhausted him. Before organizing the army at Tilbury, he had accepted the title of governor in the Netherlands, helping to fight off King Philip and his troops. After the Spanish defeat, Dudley, plagued by stomach pains and high fever, had traveled slowly to Buxton, hoping that healing waters there would revive him. He made it to his hunting lodge near Woodstock where, on September 4, 1588, he died.

At Elizabeth's moment of great triumph, she plunged into sorrow. She mourned Dudley, but few in the country shared her sorrow. Some even suggested that Dudley's wife, Lettice, had poisoned him with one of his own deadly potions in order to marry her lover. Many people believed the tale and continued to spread rumors about Dudley after his death.

Dudley was one of the few people to whom Elizabeth had truly been close. "She was so grieved that for some days she shut herself in her chamber alone and refused to speak to anyone until the Treasurer and other councilors had the door broken open and entered to see her," wrote the Spanish ambassador's agent. Elizabeth read and reread Dudley's last letter to her, written just days before he died. She wrote on it "his last letter," and kept it in a pearl-covered chest near her bed with her most precious belongings. Dudley left Elizabeth a necklace of six hundred pearls, which she wore in a painting commemorating the victory over Spain. But eventually, Elizabeth needed to put her own emotions aside and continue ruling the country.

After Dudley died, Elizabeth turned to his stepson Robert Devereaux, the second Earl of Essex. He quickly moved up in court status and became Elizabeth's new favorite. They were related—Elizabeth and his mother were cousins—and soon Elizabeth seemed to think of Essex as the son she never had. He took over his stepfather's apartments at court and was always at Elizabeth's side. Unlike Dudley, he was popular with the

Robert Dudley's trouble-making stepson, Robert Devereaux, the Earl of Essex.
(Woburn Abbey, Bedfordshire)

people, which made Elizabeth jealous. Essex believed he could shape Elizabeth to his will. He sulked, argued, and threatened to leave court and live in the country if he didn't get his wishes.

Essex's position of privilege was soon threatened by Sir Charles Blount, whom Elizabeth first saw jousting in a tournament. She sent Blount the golden queen from her chess set. He tied it to his arm with a red ribbon. When Essex noticed, he called Blount a fool. Blount challenged Essex to a duel. During the duel, he slashed Essex in the thigh and disarmed him. Although Elizabeth usually disliked dueling, she was growing weary of Essex's tantrums and arrogance. "By God's death," she said, "it was fit that someone or other should take him down, and teach him better manners, otherwise there will be no ruling of him."

In the spring of 1589, Elizabeth decided to crush Spain's naval power for good. She sent Drake, Raleigh, and Sir John Norris with 150 ships and 20,000 men to destroy the remains of the Spanish fleet. England also planned to help Portuguese patriots place Don Antonio on the throne of Portugal, overthrowing Spanish rule.

Essex was desperate to go too. Elizabeth, worried about his rash behavior and quick temper, forbid him. Early in April he ran away and persuaded Sir Roger Williams to let him come along. By the time Elizabeth discovered Essex's actions, he was already at sea. She wrote furiously to Williams, commanding him to send Essex back safely. She also wrote to Essex, complaining of his behavior. Two months later, when Elizabeth's letters caught up with the ships, the fleet was already approaching Portugal. Drake attacked, but the Portuguese rebels had failed to rise to support the invasion and the English ships were driven back. Further thwarted by severe storms at sea, the English fleet had to give up. Between 4,000-11,000 men died. Elizabeth was £49,000 poorer. The expedition was a disaster.

When the fleet returned, Elizabeth vented her anger on Drake and Norris. She rewarded Raleigh, who had fought well, with a medal, and looked the other way as Essex played the role of the returning hero. She forgave him for his disobedience.

For a short time, Elizabeth amused herself with hunting, jousting, and feasting. Looking forward to a peaceful Europe, she offered financial support to the new king of France, Henry IV. A leader in the Huguenot rebellions, he had come to power when the Catholic Henry III was assassinated. Elizabeth helped establish Henry IV firmly on the throne of France, demonstrating her power in Europe. To end France's religious wars, Henry IV converted to Catholicism, recognizing it as the religion of the French majority. He also passed the Edict of Nantes, granting civil rights and freedoms to the Huguenots. Then Henry began the process of politically rebuilding war-torn France.

For Elizabeth, these quieter times were a welcome lull. She was now fifty-six years old, and still healthy but beginning to feel her age. On April 6, 1590, her advisor Sir Francis Walsingham died. Although he had served Elizabeth faithfully for years, he was unable to pay off his debts on his meager salary. Walsingham had himself buried at night to prevent creditors from seizing his coffin. Elizabeth and all of England mourned his passing.

Eighty-two-year-old Blanche Parry, who served Elizabeth since the queen's birth, also died in 1590. She left Elizabeth without the reassuring company of herself or Kat Ashley, who had died years earlier.

In November 1591, Elizabeth's friend and advisor Sir Christopher Hatton died. It seemed as if everyone she loved was being taken away from her. She became obsessed with thoughts of death, hating anything that reminded her of it. Once, when someone placed a covered dish of food in front of her, she asked what it was. "Madame, it is a coffin," he replied. 'Coffin' was a word used to describe a pie. "Are you such a fool to give a pie such a name," she shouted. Courtiers began to avoid speaking of death around Elizabeth.

As the ranks of Elizabeth's councilors and friends thinned, a new generation of courtiers was rising up to take their places. William Cecil, Elizabeth's secretary of state, was grooming his son, Robert, to take over the position. People suggested Elizabeth was recreating the court of her youth by relying on Cecil's son and Dudley's stepson.

Other courtiers in Elizabeth's later years were occupied mainly by their own interests. Elizabeth had to adjust to a court under the influence of people younger than she. They had different tastes, ideas, and attitudes. She tried to keep peace among them, balancing the different factions.

Many of these younger courtiers and servants found Elizabeth's behavior verging on the ridiculous. The actions that appeared bold and confident in her youth

Elizabeth's trusty advisor William Cecil *(left)* with his son Robert, who successfully struggled to outmaneuver Essex for favor with the queen in her declining years.

now seemed outlandish and unfeminine. Elizabeth wore elegant clothes and flirted with men, but also swore loudly and boasted. She wore flowers in her hair but stormed through her apartments slapping her serving women and demanding to be told she was as beautiful as the sun. The ladies of the court quietly ridiculed her behind her back. The selfish, handsome Essex, whom Elizabeth nicknamed her 'Wild Horse,' led this new generation, who proudly thought they could outwit the aging queen.

Essex constantly schemed to increase his own power. He saw an opportunity to gain fame by joining the French in a war against Spain. He begged Elizabeth to let him command an army. She hesitated but relented when Henry IV requested his appointment. Essex spent his time in France entertaining guests and treated the war as a game. Elizabeth was furious and frustrated. Essex was wasting her time and money, and not keeping her informed of his plans. She ordered him home. Before Essex returned, he knighted twenty-four of his supporters, further enraging Elizabeth as only the crown had the right to create a knight. She feared Essex was building up his own base of power.

When Essex returned to England, he oozed charm. Elizabeth allowed him to return to France. His campaign ended in disaster. Three thousand men died of illness or deserted the army. Elizabeth ordered Essex home once again. Within a year, he had established a strong spy network for England. Impressed by his work, Elizabeth appointed him a Privy Councilor in 1593. She hoped advancing Essex from a private favorite to a public councilor would steady his rash behavior. Now he would have to compete with other councilors for Elizabeth's ear.

In July 1595, Spanish ships attacked Cornwall, burning Penzance and sacking the village of Mousehole. Elizabeth ordered the strengthening of England's coastal defenses. Drake suggested a raid on Panama to divert King Philip and seize more Spanish treasure. Elizabeth agreed. But when Drake's fleet returned, having accomplished nothing, it brought sad news. Drake had died from dysentery. The English hero was buried at sea.

Essex wanted to lead a campaign against Spain. After much debate, Elizabeth agreed. She appointed him and Lord Howard Effingham as joint commanders and Raleigh as Rear Admiral. They set off for Spain to raid Cadiz, where Philip II's ships were being prepared to attack England. They caught the Spanish forces by surprise, then ransacked and burned Cadiz for two weeks. Elizabeth rejoiced when she heard of the victory. Essex returned to England a hero. He had become the most popular man in the nation. Yet Elizabeth fretted about his popularity, fearing the impetuous Essex could prove to be dangerous to the aging queen and her realm.

Elizabeth was in her mid-sixties. As she grew older, people began to whisper and speculate about her successor. King James of Scotland was a popular choice among Elizabeth's subjects. A Protestant and a married man with two sons, he would carry on England's religious tradition and already had heirs. Few people desired another female ruler. Many still thought it was shameful for men to be ruled by a woman. In 1586, Elizabeth had made an alliance with James, promising him she would do nothing to prevent his claim to the English throne, unless he provoked her. But she would make no more definite reassurances. The question of succession continued to haunt Elizabeth's reign.

For a third year in a row, England suffered from rainy summers and bad harvests. People had little food and prices were high. Riots broke out. By winter, there was famine and people were dying. Elizabeth ordered the government to bring in food to feed the poor. Wednesdays and Fridays became fast days. The wealthy skipped their suppers and donated the money they saved to church parishes to help feed the hungry.

As Elizabeth dealt with England's internal problems, King Philip II continued to plan revenge for his humiliating defeats. He ordered the building of an even stronger Armada and attempted several more times to fulfill his holy crusade. But each time, he was thwarted by England or terrible storms. In 1597, Philip's proud Armada returned home in ruins once again. His commitment to religious conflict had helped bankrupt Spain, and his people were tired of this vendetta.

For years, Elizabeth had financially supported the Netherlands and France in their battles against Spain. Now the Netherlands had freed itself from Spanish control, and a strong French monarchy, hostile to Spain, helped her isolate the once-powerful kingdom.

Then, in the spring of 1598, the kings of Spain and France negotiated peace with each other. Essex thought Spain would use the peace treaties as a diversion to regroup and plan another assault on England. Others thought Spain, weakened by decades of war, was no longer a threat. Peace negotiations between England and Spain began, but inched forward as Philip and Elizabeth refused to make concessions.

Maddened that Elizabeth was considering peace with Spain, Essex became increasingly bold and unbalanced. In a heated council meeting, Essex turned his back on Elizabeth, a deliberate sign of disrespect, during their debate. "Go to the devil!" Elizabeth shouted, slapping him around his ears. "Get you gone and be hanged!"

Essex drew his sword and looked as if he might strike her. As Elizabeth stood in silence, he stormed out of the room, making threats, and then rode away.

Most people thought she would order Essex to be imprisoned in the tower. Although Elizabeth was growing wary of his refusal to play by her rules, she was blinded by her affection for him. Essex considered the queen to be in the wrong for the way she had treated him. While Elizabeth refused to speak of the incident again, Essex stayed away from court and sulked.

Elizabeth's peace negotiations with Spain eventually ground to a halt. Her Dutch allies refused to condone any treaty with Spain because of the years of Spanish cruelty they had endured. Philip II died in the fall of 1598 and his son, Philip III, vowed to continue the war against England.

Elizabeth had by now outlived many of her friends and enemies. Few in Europe could remember a time when she had not been queen of England. On August 4, 1598, William Cecil died. Elizabeth had relied on him for over half a century. The seventy-eight-year-old Cecil had represented the last remnant of her early reign. Elizabeth knew her own reign soon would come to an end but refused to accept the fact that she was aging. Each day, Elizabeth's chamber ladies helped her maintain her youthful appearance by using tricks of makeup and wigs. Elizabeth ordered the mirrors to be removed from her palaces so she could avoid seeing her own aged face.

Two weeks after Cecil died, Elizabeth learned of a

Elizabeth is ageless in this painting, known as the *Rainbow Portrait*, which was made in 1600 when the queen was in her late sixties. The portrait is currently housed at the site of Elizabeth's childhood home, now known as the Hatfield House.

rebellion against English domination in Ireland. The relationship between the Irish and the English had long been tense and it erupted into violence over plantation policy that resulted from England's attempt to populate Ireland with settlers who followed English law and customs and were loyal to the Crown. These were mostly Protestant settlers given land seized from Irish Catholic owners, provoking fierce Irish resistance.

Essex used the opportunity to get back into Elizabeth's good graces. He persuaded Elizabeth to appoint him lord lieutenant of Ireland and to create the largest army ever raised during her reign. Although she agreed to his expensive request, Essex was becoming increasingly difficult to manage. Some said Essex's "greatness was now judged to depend as much on Her Majesty's fear of him as her love of him."

Early in 1599, Essex left for Ireland. Quickly his army of 17,000 was reduced to a quarter of its size. Defying Elizabeth's orders, Essex met with the rebel leader and agreed to a truce. On September 28, caked with mud and grime, Essex burst unannounced into Elizabeth's bedchamber.

Elizabeth had just awoken. Thinking perhaps Essex had raised an army against her, she greeted him cautiously then suggested they could talk further when they were both more presentable. Essex had no idea how worried she was, or how much he had offended and embarrassed his aged queen by seeing her unwigged and unadorned by dress or jewelry. When Elizabeth realized Essex had abandoned his post, lost the crown £300,000, and made an unapproved treaty, she placed him under house arrest. He was brought before a tribunal and found guilty of all counts. Essex was relieved of all of his duties and privileges.

After a year under house arrest, Elizabeth set Essex free. Months later, he began plotting to capture Elizabeth and rule England in her name. He gathered people who held grudges against the queen and welcomed them to his house. As they plotted the coup, Essex continued to write Elizabeth oily, groveling letters.

It was a tempting time for a coup. A decade of terrible weather and bad harvests had left thousands hungry and discontented. It was said that the poor had to feed their children on "dogs, cats, and nettle roots" to keep them from starving. The poverty was so rampant that even Elizabeth sold some of her property, lands worth £800,000, and some of Henry VIII's heirlooms. Essex decided the time was ripe to seize power. He was convinced the people would follow him into rebellion.

On February 8, Essex gathered his friends and supporters. Flanked by two hundred soldiers, they swarmed through London. Essex expected people to flock to him, strengthening his numbers, but he had overestimated his popularity. People he thought would support him instead tried to block him from continuing on towards the palace. Essex realized all was lost. He fled back to his house and began burning incriminating papers.

By evening, Essex had surrendered and eighty-five of the rebels had been rounded up. He was tried, found guilty of treason, and sentenced to death. On February 25, the thirty-three-year-old Essex was beheaded. Many

The execution of the Earl of Essex after the uncovering of his plot against Elizabeth, who had given him the bulk of his power. *(Folger Shakespeare Library, Washington, D.C.)*

Londoners mourned him. Although Elizabeth often spoke of Essex with tears, she signed his death warrant and did not regret her decision. The queen and her kingdom were safer.

Elizabeth had remained strong throughout the uprising, but now she showed the strain. She kept a rusty sword with her at all times, fearing rebellion. She ate little and frequently raged at her ladies, stamping her feet at bad news. She was tired and suffering from depression and prone to fits of weeping. The queen confided to the French ambassador "she was tired of life, for nothing now contented her or gave her any enjoyment."

9

CHEATING DEATH

Elizabeth's thirteenth and final Parliament met in October of 1601. At sixty-eight years old, she had ruled England for nearly forty-three years. As Elizabeth ascended the steps to her throne, she staggered under the weight of her heavy robes and crown. Several men rushed forward to catch her before she fell. She recovered and continued the ceremony.

This Parliament had serious problems to address. Adding to the issue of famine, the population of England had increased dramatically during the years of Elizabeth's reign. Beggars were becoming a serious problem as hunger and poverty ravaged the country.

The Parliament responded by publishing the Poor Law Act, which established a program for the entire country, based on the progressive idea that no one in

England needed to starve. Instead of relying solely on private charity, care of the poor was now mandated by the government. Under this reform, local church parishes now were required by law to aid poor people in their area. Each city would have a workhouse to provide employment for the poor. Those who could afford to were required to pay taxes to help the needy. This national system of relief for the poor would last until the nineteenth century and was a huge step forward in social welfare policies.

Another problem Parliament addressed was the system of monopolies. Currently, the queen could offer royal grants to people giving them the sole right to make or sell a certain product, such as wines or salt. The grant-holders frequently abused this powerful privilege, causing inflated prices and corruption as men wrangled for the rights to control a certain trade. The House of Commons was determined to end the queen's ability to grant monopolies. Hearing her Parliament's arguments, Elizabeth decided to end the system of monopolies immediately, voluntarily limiting her powers. It was a surprising and generous move that provided great relief for her subjects.

Parliament planned to send a small group to Elizabeth expressing their gratitude for this decision, but it was discovered that each member of Parliament wanted to thank her. Elizabeth accepted them all at Whitehall Palace. As they knelt before her, Elizabeth made what became known as her Golden Speech. These were her

Elizabeth, surrounded by her advisors and the officials of her government, meets with Parliament at Whitehall Palace. *(Hulton Archive / Getty Images)*

farewell words to her beloved subjects. Elizabeth spoke before them as an aged, frail woman, her red wig covering her thinning hair, her face covered with white powder and rouge:

I do assure you, there is no prince that loves his
subjects better. There is no jewel, be it of never so rich
a price, which I set before this jewel: I mean your love.
For I do more esteem it than any treasure or riches, for
those we know how to prize; but loyalty, love and
thanks—I account them invaluable. . . . To be a king
and wear a crown is more glorious to them that see it
than it is a pleasure to them that bear it. And for my
part, were it not for conscience's sake to discharge the
duty that God hath laid upon me, and to maintain His
Glory and keep you in safety, in mine own disposition
I should be willing to resign the place I hold to any
other, and glad to be free of the glory with the labours;
for it is not my desire to live nor reign longer than my
life and reign shall be for your good. And though you
have had and may have many mightier and wiser
princes sitting in this seat, yet you never had nor shall
have any that love you better.

Although Elizabeth was growing weary, she still began
each day with a brisk walk in the garden. She hunted and
danced and took great pleasure in physically surpassing
men and women half her age. Her physicians said if old
age didn't kill her, all this exertion surely would. But
Elizabeth had outlived several personal physicians. Once,
the queen was glimpsed through a window dancing
alone to a dance called the Spanish Panic. Elizabeth
moved quickly to the music, stamping her feet in rhythm,
tossing her head, defying death.

During their previous summer progress, many of the
courtiers had complained about the thought of another

long journey. Elizabeth, who still enjoyed these trips, told "the old to stay behind and the young and able to go with her." Elizabeth always loved being able to do what people told her she could not.

In September, as Elizabeth moved from Hampton Court to London, a storm blew in, drenching everything with rain. The roads became a string of muddy potholes. The hard rain bounced off the canvas-covered wagons. Elizabeth planned to make the journey on horseback, as she usually did. "It is not meet [appropriate] for one of your majesty's years to ride in such a storm," said Henry Hunsdon, the son of Elizabeth's former Lord Chamberlain. "My years!" Elizabeth said, glaring at him. "Maids, to your horses quickly!" She mounted her horse and rode off before anyone could stop her, not pausing until she reached London.

Elizabeth exercised relentlessly for other reasons besides health. She had always been aware of maintaining the image of strength and invulnerability. King James of Scotland and all of the other European monarchs heard about every pain or sign of weakness she showed through their ambassadors and spies. Elizabeth knew she needed to display her physical strength to contradict any rumors. Driving out in her jewel-covered carriage, pulled by horses whose manes and tails were dyed as bright orange as her own wig, she waved and called to her subjects.

Elizabeth's determined efforts to conceal even minor pains sometimes bordered on the comical. She went to

Elizabeth in her late sixties, in a painting by the Flemish artist Marcus Gheeraerts the Younger.

great lengths to call her good health to people's attention. Robert Cecil once told a friend, "The Queen hath a desperate ache in her right thumb, but will not be known of it, nor the gout it cannot be, nor dare it be."

To a certain extent, Elizabeth's attempts at maintaining her youthful image succeeded. But there were those close to her willing to tell informers the real story. After an hour's ride, she had to stay in bed for two days to recuperate. Elizabeth frequently took naps during the day to keep up her strength. The youthful image she demanded became increasingly difficult to conjure up. She needed help dismounting from her horse and used a walking stick when climbing steep steps. Sometimes the queen accepted help; other times she impatiently refused it.

After Essex's execution, Elizabeth became unpredictable. She frequently had tantrums in front of her ladies-in-waiting. She would break into a fury if she discovered a marriage, either planned or accomplished, that she had not approved. Elizabeth often asked her ladies if they wished to marry one day. To avoid angering her, they knew to say no. Yet for all the rumors of her pettiness and irritability, Elizabeth still had the power to exercise her charm and grace, whether it was chatting in Italian with an envoy from Venice or teasing her courtiers over their latest love interests.

The fall of 1602 was brightened by good news. The harvest had been bountiful. The plague, which had run rampant during the summer, receded. Ireland was momentarily calm. But Elizabeth's eyesight was failing, and she had become absentminded. She frequently shouted hoarsely at her servants for forgetting things, when she herself had forgotten them. She sometimes sent for people and then was furious when they arrived, not remembering she had sent for them.

Cecil and her councilors managed Elizabeth's anger the best they could. They read letters aloud to her and avoiding giving her bad news at night so she could sleep better. They quieted her worries by sometimes misrepresenting affairs in small ways. Elizabeth still worked late into the night. She bent over letters, squinting in the firelight to read them, before she signed her name on the bottom, her handwriting now spidery.

Throughout her reign, Elizabeth had inspired love, awe, and respect in the hearts of her subjects. During the Elizabethan era, England had experienced the greatest cultural renaissance in the country's history. New commercial contacts with Europe and the rest of the world fueled changes and innovations in poetry, painting, music, and architecture. Poetry had one of its most creative, prolific periods under masters such as William Shakespeare and Edmund Spenser. Innovative forms of verse and exploration of new rhyme schemes and topics characterized this great flowering of English literature.

By the end of Elizabeth's reign, England and all of Western Europe had become more literate. The Reformation had played a tremendous role as Protestant reformers insisted that individuals read the Bible in their own languages. Reading and writing no longer were a privilege of the elite. By the end of the sixteenth century, people had everything from almanacs to love stories available to them.

New scientific knowledge could be made available in print quickly, sparking the spread of ideas and communication. This led to advances in anatomy, astronomy, physics, and other disciplines. Sir Francis Bacon penned essays about experimentation and scientific method. In 1543, the Polish scholar Nicholas Copernicus had created the first model of the solar system with the sun at the center, rather than the Earth, supporting his theory with detailed measurements and experiments. Ideas about the universe and man's place in it were being reshaped. Educated Europeans were in a different mental world than they had been just fifty years before.

English people had developed a growing national pride, due in part to England's exploration, trade expansion, and fledgling colonies in the Americas. The defeat of Spain's mighty Armada had launched a new era of England as a sea power. English people were prouder, wealthier, and more abundant. The population of England had doubled since 1520 and was now over four million.

Elizabeth's adventurers had been just some of the many European explorers sailing the seas and exploring the New World, leading to advances in navigation, geography, and the sciences. People's eyes had been opened to the world beyond Europe's borders. Europeans were armed with an expanding knowledge about those faraway places, and ready to explore the vast opportunities that waited. Control of trade and colonization would be the next battleground for Europe, and the claims were often settled by sea power.

The balance of power had changed in Europe since Elizabeth took her coronation oath. At the beginning of

Sixteenth-century exploration created an increasingly complex worldview. Maps such as this one demonstrate a newly detailed understanding of the non-European world.

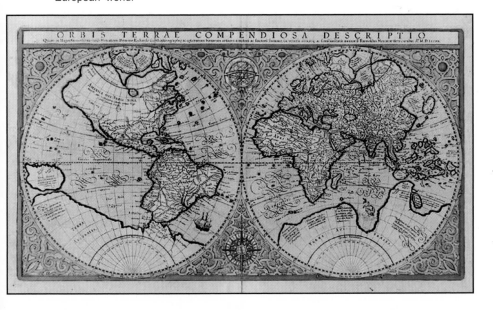

her reign, her realm had been an insular state, surrounded by enemies. Now England was a strong power in Western Europe, flanked by allies in Scotland, France, and the Netherlands. England could count herself as one of these now-stable states. Elizabeth's religious tolerance had helped to minimize the religious turmoil that shattered other nations, such as France, in the sixteenth century. Elizabeth's reign had been long and glorious, but it was drawing to an end.

In January 1603, Elizabeth caught a cold as the court moved to Richmond Palace. Elizabeth called the palace "a warm winter box for her old age." But as the dark, rainy month wore on, her cold worsened into bronchitis. By February, she was much weaker, with a fever and a sore throat. She refused any medicines and sat on the floor on embroidered cushions staring at one spot for hours. The worst of all of her symptoms was the depression that came from realizing she could not win this battle. Her coronation ring had to be cut off her finger, as it was cutting into her swollen flesh. The ring symbolized her marriage to England; its removal seemed to be an omen.

By the first days of March, Elizabeth was still sitting on her floor cushions, refusing to change her clothes, neither eating nor sleeping. One day she had her servants lift her onto a low chair. When Elizabeth couldn't rise from it herself, she commanded servants to help her to stand. Once upright, Elizabeth stood there for fifteen hours, determined to defy death. Watched helplessly by

Paul Delaroche's nineteenth-century painting depicts Elizabeth on her deathbed, surrounded by her courtiers and servants. *(Courtesy of Art Resource.)*

her courtiers, she finally fainted back onto her cushions.

On March 21, Elizabeth allowed her servants to change her clothes and put her to bed. Covered with embroidered sheets, she lay staring up at the ornate beasts carved on her high wooden bed, her head on a silk pillow. A swelling in her throat broke open and within a few hours, she could no longer speak. Voices murmured in her room and across her realm as prayers and meditations were read. Her musicians played softly to soothe her. Late in the evening of March 23, Elizabeth turned her face towards the wall and fell asleep. Several hours later, in the early morning of March 24, 1603, the doctor pronounced the sixty-nine-year-old queen dead.

Elizabeth had lived longer than any English ruler before her. Her reign had seen political perils, money woes, crises, natural disasters, plots real and imagined, and foreign enemies massing for attack. Throughout it all, she had doggedly refused to name her successor. Although King James of Scotland had not officially been named Elizabeth's successor, everyone understood he would be the next to wear the English crown. A horse stood saddled and waiting in the palace's courtyard to carry the news of Elizabeth's death to Scotland.

One of Elizabeth's ladies removed a sapphire ring from the queen's finger, as had been prearranged. She dropped it through the window to her brother, Robert Carey, who was waiting below. He mounted the horse and galloped off into the dark rain to spread the news of Queen Elizabeth's death. When King James received the ring, he would know Elizabeth's glorious reign had come to a close.

The next morning, in London, James was proclaimed king of England. The Elizabethan age was over. At first, Elizabeth's subjects were quiet with the weight of her death. "I think the sorrow for her Majesty's departure was so deep in many hearts, they could not so suddenly show any great joy," said one Londoner. But by that evening, bonfires were lit in celebration and bells rang in honor of their new king. James would rule until 1625, but religious and civil troubles would plague England through the seventeenth century.

For the first few days after her death, Elizabeth's body lay at Richmond, nearly forgotten in the initial excitement over the new monarch. Soon after, Elizabeth was wrapped in cloth and enclosed in a lead coffin. Her coffin was taken to Whitehall Palace at night, on a torchlit barge draped in black velvet. She lay in state, visited by lords and ladies, until her funeral on April 28. Elizabeth's

Elizabeth's successor, James I.

coffin was carried on a chariot, drawn by four horses covered in black velvet. Her lords, councilors, courtiers, and servants followed. Colorful banners fluttered and trumpets sounded. Thousands lined the funeral route and wept for their lost queen.

Elizabeth was buried in Westminster Abbey. Her coffin was placed over her sister Mary's in the Tudor vault. Elizabeth was the last surviving member of the Tudor family, and so the vault was sealed. A magnificent white marble sculpture was erected to her memory.

Timeline

1533   Elizabeth Tudor is born at Greenwich Palace in London, England, on September 7.

1536   Her mother, Anne Boleyn, is executed.

1547   Father, King Henry VIII dies; half brother Edward VI ascends the throne.

1553   Edward dies; Lady Jane Grey is crowned; Elizabeth's half sister Mary seizes the throne.

1554   Thomas Wyatt leads a rebellion; Elizabeth is imprisoned in the Tower of London for two months.

1558   Queen Mary dies and Elizabeth succeeds her.

1559   Elizabeth is officially crowned on January 15; the Treaty of Cateau-Cambrésis initiates peace between England and France.

1560   Treaty of Edinburgh is signed, ending French occupation of Scotland.

1562   Elizabeth contracts smallpox.

1566   A son, James, is born to Mary Queen of Scots.

1577   Francis Drake sets out to circumnavigate the globe.

1587   Mary Queen of Scots is executed on Elizabeth's order.

1588   The Spanish Armada is defeated; Robert Dudley dies.

1601   Essex leads an unsuccessful revolt against Elizabeth.

1603   Elizabeth dies on March 24.

Sources

CHAPTER ONE: A Lonely Princess

p. 18, "Let them grumble . . ." Carolly Erickson, *Mistress Anne* (New York: St. Martin's Press, 1984), 178.

p. 18, "Hot . . . but not . . ." David Starkey, *Elizabeth: The Struggle for the Throne* (New York: Harper Collins, 2001), 4.

p. 19, "knew of no. . ." Anne Somerset, *Elizabeth I* (New York: St. Martin's Press, 1991), 4.

p. 22, "had never . . ." Erickson, *Mistress Anne,* 258.

p. 24, "ancient and sad . . ." Carolly Erickson, *The First Elizabeth* (New York: St. Martin's Press, 1983), 41.

p. 26, "ill luck . . ." Alison Plowden, *The House of Tudor,* (Phoenix Mill, UK: Sutton), 147.

p. 29, "the brightest star . . ." Alison Weir, *Elizabeth the Queen* (London: Jonathan Cape, 1998), 14.

p. 34, "He is a wonderful . . ." Carolly Erickson, *Bloody Mary* (New York: St. Martin's Press, 1978), 225.

p. 34, "She prides herself . . ." Somerset, *Elizabeth I,* 15.

CHAPTER TWO: Trapped

p. 41, "The crown is not . . ." Alison Weir, *The Children of Henry VIII* (New York: Ballantine Books, 1996), 165.

p. 44, "Everyone believes . . ." Weir, *The Children of Henry VIII,* 214.

p. 44, "bring about . . ." Somerset, *Elizabeth I*, 37.

p. 47, "without peril . . ." Starkey, *Struggle for the Throne,* 136.

p. 49, "If anyone ever did . . ." Erickson, *The First Elizabeth*, 124.

p. 51, "Much suspected, by me . . ." Christopher Hibbert, *The Virgin Queen: Elizabeth I, Genius of the Golden Age* (Reading, MA: Addison-Wesley, 1991), 53.

p. 53, *"A Domine factum . . ."* Somerset, *Elizabeth I,* 57.

CHAPTER THREE: A Kingdom in Shambles

p. 56, "God save . . ." Erickson, *The First Elizabeth,* 177.

p. 56, "If ever any . . ." Somerset, *Elizabeth I,* 65.

p. 57, "The burden . . ." Ibid., 59.

p. 62, "The Queen poor . . ." Jane Resh Thomas, *Behind the Mask: The Life of Queen Elizabeth I* (New York: Clarion Books, 1998), 82.

p. 63, "My sex cannot diminish . . ." Somerset, *Elizabeth I,* 60.

p. 63, "the eyes . . ." Ibid., 66.

p. 66, "more feared than . . ." Lacey Baldwin Smith, *The Elizabethan World* (Boston: Houghton Mifflin, 1967), 71.

CHAPTER FOUR: Love and Politics

p. 73, "The Queen is . . ." Weir, *Elizabeth the Queen,* 25.

p. 73, "relieved of the pains . . ." Somerset, *Elizabeth I,* 90.

p. 75, "that a Queen . . ." Hibbert, *Virgin Queen*, 78.

p. 75, "I am already bound . . ." Weir, *Elizabeth the Queen,* 44.

p. 76, "Princes . . . transact . . ." Somerset, *Elizabeth I,* 60.

p. 79, "To say the truth . . ." Erickson, *The First Elizabeth,* 184.

p. 81, "The Queen of England . . ." Baldwin Smith, *The Elizabethan World,* 72.

p. 81, "I will have . . ." Somerset, *Elizabeth I,* 138.

p. 82, "Last night the people . . ." Peter Brimacombe, *All the Queen's Men* (New York: St. Martin's Press, 2000), 41.

p. 85, "God help England . . ." Somerset, *Elizabeth I,* 160.

CHAPTER FIVE: Good Queen Bess

p. 90-91, "There is a strong idea . . ." Wallace MacCaffrey, *Elizabeth I* (New York: Oxford University Press, 1993), 93.

p. 93, "I lack . . ." Somerset, *Elizabeth I,* 335.

p. 93, "I do not . . ." Hibbert, *Virgin Queen,* 80.

CHAPTER SIX: Rebellion

p. 112, "Elizabeth, the pretended . . ." Somerset, *Elizabeth I,* 245.

p. 114, "the worst woman . . ." Ibid., 397.

p. 115, "one of the greatest . . ." John A. Wagner, *Historical Dictionary of the Elizabethan World: Britain, Ireland, Europe, and America* (Phoenix, AZ: Oryx Press, 1999), 268.

p. 117, "I have always . . ." Erickson, *The First Elizabeth,* 314.

p. 117, "You may write this . . ." Brimacombe, *Queen's Men,* 116.

p. 118, "If I cannot . . ." Erickson, *The First Elizabeth,* 329.

p. 121, "the serpent . . ." Ibid., 363.

p. 122, "It is very fine . . ." Weir, *Elizabeth the Queen,* 381.

p. 122, "miserable accident," Ibid., 381.

p. 123, "I never saw . . ." Somerset, *Elizabeth I,* 440.

CHAPTER SEVEN: War with Spain

p. 127, "singe the King. . ." Hibbert, *Virgin Queen,* 220.

p. 134-135, "I have placed . . . in the field," Smith, *The Elizabethan World,* 203-204.

p. 135, "so inflamed the hearts . . ." Weir, *Elizabeth the Queen,* 394.

p. 137, "She came . . ." Erickson, *The First Elizabeth,* 377.

p. 137, "She certainly is . . ." Plowden, *House of Tudor,* 283.

p. 137, "The rose is red . . ." Baldwin Smith, *The Elizabethan World,* 76.

CHAPTER EIGHT: Treasures and Treason

p. 139, "She was so grieved . . ." Somerset, *Elizabeth I,* 468.

p. 141, "By God's death . . ." Ibid., 476.

p. 143, "Madame, it is . . ." Weir, *Elizabeth the Queen,* 411.

p. 147, "Go to the devil . . ." Ibid., 434.

p. 150, "greatness was now . . ." Ibid., 440.

p. 151, "dogs, cats . . ." Erickson, *The First Elizabeth,* 397.

p. 152, "she was tired . . ." Weir, *Elizabeth the Queen,* 470.

CHAPTER NINE: Cheating Death

p. 156, "I do assure you . . ." Ibid., 473-474.

p. 157, "the old . . ." Ibid., 263.

p. 157, "It is not meet . . ." Erickson, *The First Elizabeth,* 403.

p. 157, "My years . . ." Ibid.

p. 158, "The Queen hath . . ." Somerset, *Elizabeth I,* 554.

p. 162, "a warm winter . . ." Erickson, *The First Elizabeth,* 405.

p. 164, "I think . . ." Ibid., 568.

Bibliography

Brimacombe, Peter. *All the Queen's Men.* New York: St. Martin's Press, 2000.

Davies, Norman. *Europe: A History.* New York: Oxford University Press, 1996.

Erickson, Carolly. *Bloody Mary.* New York: St. Martin's Press, 1978.

———. *Mistress Anne.* New York: St. Martin's Press, 1984.

———. *The First Elizabeth.* New York: St. Martin's Press, 1983.

Fraser, Antonia. *Mary Queen of Scots.* New York: Dell, 1969.

———. *The Wives of Henry VIII.* New York: Knopf, 1992.

Hart, Roger. *English Life in Tudor Times.* New York: G. P. Putnam's Sons, 1972.

Hibbert, Christopher. *The Virgin Queen: Elizabeth I, Genius of the Golden Age.* Reading, MA: Addison-Wesley, 1991.

MacCaffrey, Wallace. *Elizabeth I.* New York: Oxford University Press, 1993.

Plowden, Alison. *The House of Tudor.* Phoenix Mill, UK: Sutton, 1998.

Pritchard, R.E. *Shakespeare's England: Life in Elizabethan and Jacobean Times.* Phoenix Mill, UK: Sutton, 1999.

Slavin, Arthur. *The Tudor Age and Beyond: England from the Black Death to the End of the Age of Elizabeth.* Malabar, FL: Robert E. Krieger, 1987.

Smith, Lacey Baldwin. *The Elizabethan World.* Boston: Houghton Mifflin, 1967.

Somerset, Anne. *Elizabeth I.* New York: St. Martin's Press, 1991.

Starkey, David. *Elizabeth: The Struggle for the Throne.* New York: Harper Collins, 2001.

Thomas, Jane Resh. *Behind the Mask: The Life of Queen Elizabeth I.* New York: Clarion Books, 1998.

Wagner, John A. *Historical Dictionary of the Elizabethan World: Britain, Ireland, Europe, and America.* Phoenix, AZ: Oryx Press, 1999.

Weir, Alison. *Elizabeth the Queen.* London: Jonathan Cape, 1998.

———. *The Children of Henry VIII.* New York: Ballantine Books, 1996.

———. *The Six Wives of Henry VIII.* New York: Ballantine Books, 1991.

Web sites

http://www.royal.gov.uk
The official Web site of the British monarchy. These pages contain information about the history of the monarchy, including a complete listing of the kings and queens of England and Britain, with brief biographies.

http://www.elizabethi.org
A Web site devoted to Elizabeth I's life, times, and reign.

http://englishhistory.net/tudor/monarchs/eliz1.html
These pages offer pictures of the queen and her court as well as poems and speeches written by Elizabeth.

http://www.nps.gov/fora/roanokerev.htm
Hosted by the National Parks Service, these interesting and informative pages explore the history of the Roanoke settlement and the early colonization of America, both heavily determined by Elizabethan expansion.

Index